Man of the River

Memoir of a Brown Water Sailor
in Vietnam, 1968-1969

Jimmy R. Bryant
SMC USN Ret.

D1600277

Sergeant Kirkland's
Fredericksburg, Virginia

Published & Distributed by

Sergeant Kirkland's Museum and Historical Society, Inc.

912 Lafayette Blvd., Fredericksburg, Virginia 22401-5617
Tel. (540) 899-5565; Fax: (540) 899-7643
E-mail: Civil-War@msn.com

Manufactured in the USA

The paper in this book meets the guidelines
for permanence and durability of the Com-
mittee on Production Guidelines for Book
Longevity of the Council on Library Re-
sources, Inc.

Library of Congress Cataloging-in-Publication Data

Man of the River: Memoir of a Brown Water Sailor
in Vietnam, 1968-1969
p.   cm.
Includes bibliographical references (p.)
ISBN 1-887901-23-X (alk. paper)

1. Vietnamese Conflict, 1961-1975 -- Riverine Opera-
tions, American. 2. Tet Offensive, 1968. 3. Vietnamese
Conflict, 1961-1975 -- Personal Narratives, American. 4.
Bryant, Jimmy R., 1936-   . I. Title.
DS558.7.B79   1998
959.704'345

                          98-25602
                          CIP

      1 2 3 4 5 6 7 8 9 10

Cover design and page layout
by Ronald R. Seagrave

Ashes of Soldiers

Again a verse for sake of you,
*   You soldiers in the ranks--you Volunteers,*
*   Who bravely fighting, silent fell,*
*   To fill unmention'd graves.*

ASHES of soldiers!
*   As I muse, retrospective, murmuring a chant in thought,*
*   Lo! the war resumes--again to my sense your shapes,*
*   And again the advance of armies.*

*   Noiseless as mists and vapors,*
*   From their graves in the trenches ascending,*
*   From the cemeteries all through Virginia and Tennessee,*
*   From every point of the compass, out of the countless un-*
*   named graves,*
*   In wafted clouds, in myriads large, or squads of twos or*
*   threes, or single ones, they come,*
*   And silently gather round me*
*   Now sound no note, O trumpeters!*
*   Not at the head of my cavalry, parading on spirited*
*   horses,*
*   With sabres drawn and glist'ning, and carbines by their*
*   thighs--(ah, my brave horsemen!*
*   My handsome, tan-faced horsemen! what life, what joy*
*   and pride,*
*   With all the perils, were yours!)*

*   Nor you drummers--neither at reveille, at dawn,*
*   Nor the long roll alarming the camp--nor even the muf-*
*   fled beat for a burial;*
*   Nothing from you, this time, O drummers, bearing my*
*   warlike drums.*

*   But aside from these, and the marts of wealth, and the*
*   crowded promenade,*
*   Admitting around me comrades close, unseen by the rest,*
*   and voiceless*

The slain elate and alive again--the dust and debris alive,
I chant this chant of my silent soul, in the name of all
dead soldiers.

Faces so pale, with wondrous eyes, very dear, gather closer
yet; Draw close, but speak not.

Phantoms of countless lost!
Invisible to the rest, henceforth become my companions!
Follow me ever! desert me not, while I live.

Sweet are the blooming cheeks of the living! sweet are the
musical voices sounding!
But sweet, ah sweet, are the dead, with their silent eyes.

Dearest comrades! all is over and long gone;
But love is not over--and what love, O comrades!
Perfume from battle-fields rising--up from foetor arising.

Perfume therefore my chant, O love! immortal Love!
Give me to bathe the memories of all dead soldiers,
Shroud them, embalm them, cover them all over with ten-
der pride!

Perfume all! make all wholesome!
Make these ashes to nourish and blossom,
O love! O chant! solve all, fructify all with the last chem-
istry.

Give me exhaustless--make me a fountain,
That I exhale love from me wherever I go, like a moist per-
ennial dew, for the ashes of all dead soldiers.

From Walt Whitman's
1900 edition of *Leaves of Grass.*

Whitman was a Union soldier during the American Civil War.

Man of the River

Memoir of a Brown Water Sailor
in Vietnam, 1968-1969

Jimmy R. Bryant SMC USN

A fast responding PBR cuts through the water of the Bassac River in the Delta on the way to an operation Game Warden Patrol in June 1968. (Photographed by Lt. T.S. Storck, USN; US Naval Historical Center)

TABLE OF CONTENTS

Please note that the maps in this book, and their
numbered locations correspond with the "Chap-
ter Numbers."

USS Harnett County [LST-821] anchored in the Vamco Dong River just south of Ben Luc. Prior to the base being built, the ship provided a base for operations, communications and logistical support for the river patrol forces patrolling the rivers. (Official US Navy photo by PH3 Steve Howk, USN)

ACKNOWLEDGEMENTS

A number of people encouraged me to write this book. However, it was only initiated after my wife, Dorothy, had found me one night studying my old navy records that I began this task. She suggested that I write this true story, for the sake our children and grandchildren. While Dorothy feels too close to the stresses that the war placed on our family, she told me, she believes our children, and that others needed to understand what it really means when "Daddy goes to War."

Next are the naval personnel I was privilege to be stationed with while serving with the River Patrol Force. I have retained their actual names in the combat reports since this is an historical document--not fiction. I only hope they will be pleased to read about their part in the events that I record here.

Thanks to Ralph Fries, CWO-3 USN Ret., for allowing me to use some of his personal photographs of a PBR 750. Also I express my gratitude to the US Naval Historical Foundation for searching out, and providing me with, relevant photos. A special thanks to Darryl Hutchison EN2, one of my boat crew members for the use of his photos. Hutch is an eyewitness and took part in much of what is recorded here.

Here I salute my former commanding officer of the *USS Greenwood* [DE-679], Richard L. Schreadley. His authoritative book *From the Rivers to the Sea. The United States Navy in Vietnam* (1992) has served me as a reference work and as a confirmation of things I knew to be true from experience. Also useful are the internet web pages, sites and links concerning the Vietnam War, for example, "Vietnam Organizations and Support Groups," "US Navy in Vietnam," "US Navy Lost and Found Listings," and "Mobile Riverine Force in the Vietnam War."

Thanks, too, to Ronald R. Seagrave, historian and archivist, Managing Director and Administrator of Sergeant

Kirkland's Museum and Historical Society in Fredericksburg, Virginia. Ron encouraged me every step of the way, attempting to make this a better book. For his foresight and for his patience, I express my gratitude.

Finally, but certainly not least, I thank Almighty God for protecting me and my boat crews from death while serving with the River Patrol Force in Vietnam. I am now able to write about my time in this war, believing that the present generation--and those to come--are ready to read the "diary" of a Man of the River from 1968 and 1969.

DEDICATION

This book concerns my tour of duty with the River Patrol Force in Vietnam from 1968 to 1969, the time of greatest activity for the "Men of the Rivers." Until recently, we were virtual blank pages in military history. But judging by the recent flood of studies--including a cover story in the magazine *Vietnam* (2/96: "Patrol Boat Action")-- our time seems to have come. To this history, this great story, I want to add my own small memoir. No war story is a story of individuals, of course. I was part of a proud unit, Task Force 116, River Division 591. It is to my fellow patrolmen that my book is dedicated. My words are intended to honor, not only the men of Task Force 116 (Game Warden), but also Task Forces 115 (Market Time), 117 (Mobile Riverine Force)--and indeed all the Men of the Rivers, in whatever division of the Brown Water Navy they honorably served. You are not forgotten.

I attempt here, as an eyewitness, to set down an accurate record of events. I strive to be fair, but with a clear bias toward the gallant men who navigated the Asian waters with me. Although patrol reports and maps in the Appendix support my narrative account, offering a fuller picture of the patrol experience in the Brown Water Navy, I make no attempt in the main body of my memoir to offer a comprehensive account of every military operation of the river patrols in my theatre of action. That kind of history is the turf of the professional military historian and is therefore beyond the scope of this book. My words comprise a memoir--an episodical account of my experiences and impressions. I hope whatever has been lost to memory is compensated for by the distance, and perspective, that thirty years provide. The feeling of love for my comrades has not dimmed, nor have two emotions that accompanied me everywhere on the rivers: surprise and sudden terror. No preparation, and no military briefing, could insulate me from either. I only hope that my story, by virtue of its immediacy, will allow the reader to share in my recollections.

I am often asked about the feelings my crews and I had for each other. They were all exceptional men. They got angry if one of our crew got hurt; and every man felt protective of the others, regardless of color or creed. It made no difference what state or city my buddies came from. On patrol we were all family, while respecting the rank and authority of the others. During that stressful and often insane time we were able to transcend race, region and religion, for one reason because a firefight made us all equal. It is surprising how the desire to stay alive can so fully activate a sense of democracy.

Finally, I apologize for being unable to remember all the names of the men I went to war with. I feel, however, that they will know who they are and how they relate to the events recorded here. Every patrol officer, boat captain and crewmember of the PBRs (patrol boat, river) in the river patrol forces had similar stories to tell--some more dramatic, and heroic than these. Our units worked closely with the Monitors, RAG boats, Tango boats, PCFs, Zippos and other Riverine assault forces patrolling the rivers of South Vietnam. Solid support came from the sky: helicopter gunships, AC-130 gunships, OV-10A Broncos, F-100 Super Sabres, F-105 Thunder Chiefs. On the ground, the ever-vigilant US army fire bases provided artillery. We thought of ourselves as the blue-collar warriors, dressed in green uniforms and fighting the war face-to-face with the enemy.

Men of the Rives: I salute you, and say here that it was an honor to serve with you. Both the now living, and dead have upheld the finest traditions of the United States Navy. You are all Men of Valor.

FOREWORD

by
William C. McDonald, Ph.D.

John Ketwig, author of the acerbic Vietnam memoir
...*And a Hard Rain Fell*, remarks in the Introduction to his
book in 1985: "In January of 1982, there were no books
about Vietnam on our shelves... Today the Vietnam books
spill out of my closet, out from under the dresser, and across
the stereo cabinet" (xi). One wonders how Ketwig would
react to the deluge of material on Vietnam since 1985, including a stirring VHS video on the Brown Water Navy:
"River Patrol. The Game Wardens of Vietnam" (Frederickson and Tully: Brown Water Productions, 1993). Vietnam
seems to be everywhere. Books appear monthly; the *Military
Book Club* regularly features titles on Vietnam; the bi-
monthly periodical Vietnam is flourishing; computer web
pages address every aspect, and theatre, of the war; accesso-
ries, memorabilia and clothing of the war are now valued
collectibles; newsletters have wide circulation; and travel
bureaus are furiously competing with each other in offering
tours of Vietnam--scenic, cultural, historical, study, and
military--all with Vietnam veterans' discount(!). (Vets will
be surprised, and not a little sad, to see that Saigon has been
renamed Ho Chi Minh City.) Certainly no combatant,
thinking back to the late 1960s and early 1970s, would be
prepared for the America of the late 1990s, which revels in
memories of the Vietnam War. For proof, one need only go
to any library and gaze at the vast walls of books on the conflict. Whoever would have imagined that Harvard University, a bastion of the anti-war movement, would proudly list
"America and Vietnam" as its second most popular course in
a single school term? And who could have believed that the
internet, under various codes, for example,
http://grunt.space.swri.edu/index.htm, or under the words
Mobile+Riverine+Force+in+the+Vietnam+War, would

serve as the new front for web pages, links and sites for many thousands of people interested in the War--almost as many who fought it in the first place?

Vietnam is a "hot topic," so says a very recent *New York Times Book Review*. To this so-called hot topic, Jimmy R. Bryant, a Bronze Star Medal holder in charge of PBRs, adds his own gentle and modest voice. Patrol Officer Bryant, now retired as a 70% disabled veteran, waited almost exactly thirty years to speak; we are grateful he has done so. For he has an important story to tell, one filled with quiet heroism, duty, honor and love. The love he and his men share is for country and for each other. I am inspired by his tale and am pleased he has chosen to tell it in a period that promises to be remembered as the Decade of Vietnam in book publishing and historical re-evaluation -- the 1990s. Three decades provide the breathing space, and the security of reflective distance, to appraise objectively the role that US Navy patrol vessels played in a conflict that, finally and thankfully, promises to elicit more light than heat. In the 1990s scholars, military historians, popular historians, and military eye-witnesses can tell their stories at a remove from a war that seemed as present in the United States as it was on any foreign soil. Finally, even the quiet university campuses seem ready to listen, as men like Jimmy Bryant tell it "like it was."

Born in North Carolina, Jimmy Bryant was raised on a farm in the tobacco belt. He joined the US Navy in 1954 at the age of 18. After recruit training in San Diego, he served on six US Navy ships at sea; he had two shore duty assignments. His second ship was the *USS Boxer* CVS-21, converted to LPH-4, which was involved in the Nuclear Test Series of 1958 in the Pacific. His memoir covers his tour in Vietnam with River Division 591. While on active duty in Vietnam, Bryant is credited with 38 contacts with the enemy in which shots were fired. Often he stood, clearly exposed to enemy fire. His Bronze Star Medal, with Combat "V," from the year 1970 is made out to "Chief Signalman Jimmy R. Bryant, United States Navy, for Meritorious Service from October 1968 to September 1969." (Vice Admiral E.R.

Zumwalt, Jr., Commander of US Naval Forces in Vietnam spells out Chief Bryant's acts of heroism) Bryant, after recovering from injuries received in Vietnam, finished up his last tour as Company Commander at the Naval Air Technical Training Center in Millington, Tennessee.

Jimmy Bryant's memoir begins in October, 1968, the year of the Tet Offensive. (In January of that year, there was a combined assault on US positions by the NVA (North Vietnam Army) and the Viet Cong. Between Tet and his arrival in Saigon, Chief Bryant was stationed aboard the *USS Hummingbird* MSC-192, a coastal minesweeper out of Little Creek, Va. The Navy circulated a Major Call, a memorandum, looking for qualified men to join the River Patrol Force in Vietnam. Of this Force, Lt. Col. Victor Croizat has written: "(It was created) in September 1965 to patrol island waterways, to deny them to communist insurgents and enforce the curfew. The US Navy River Patrol Force, code name 'Game Warden', was designated Task Force 116 and placed under the naval component of the US Military Assistance Command, Vietnam" (Brown Water Navy, 142). In 1968 Bryant volunteered to join the River Patrol Force, and after a few weeks received orders to proceed for PBR (=patrol boat, river) training at Vallejo, California. After his unit had familiarized itself with the relevant boats, weapons and tactics, Bryant was sent to Whidbey Island, Washington, for survival training. This was followed by Vietnamese language training in San Diego. In late 1968, aircraft then brought the future brown water sailors to Vietnam, by way of Alaska and Japan. Bryant's manuscript begins upon his arrival in Saigon. It ends in 1969, the year in which President Nixon had begun a slow withdrawal of US ground troops from Vietnam.

By sheer coincidence Jimmy Bryant's memoir appears very close in time to the comprehensive book by Gordon L. Rottman, *The Vietnam Brown Water Navy: Riverine and Coastal Warfare 1965-69* (1997). Rottman begins by reminding us that the Mekong Delta is the world's largest river delta. "The Delta's real roads are its waterways," he continues, "with sampans the main mode of transportation. Even villages were either floating, built on stilts, or with individual homes on earth mounds. Malaria and dengue fever is rampant year around as are leeches, poisonous snakes, and vicious ants. The water is unfit to drink. During the dry season, December to March, salt water intrudes 20-50 miles inland up the waterways. The April to November wet, or monsoon season, brings over eighty inches of rain. Temperatures are in the 80-100F range with equally high humidity. Soldiers on foot in the Delta were exhausted after three days in the field and required at least two days to recover from constantly wet feet. Longer duration operations led to immersion foot, rashes and skin ulcers" (4).

Since the earliest times riverine and coastal warfare had long been practiced in the Vietnam Delta--by the ancient Vietnamese, Chinese, Khmers, and the modern French navy. In 1965, because of a deteriorating military situation, the US military decided to commit an American riverine force to the Delta. Army and Navy joined troops, and worked together, to develop the Mobile Riverine Force, whose mission was to interdict the flow of men and materials to the enemy. The Force started to dissolve in the summer of 1969, Rottman says, as US forces began the withdrawal from Vietnam (4).

The role of the US Navy was to patrol the many rivers in small boats that could travel the waterways at high speeds, using hit-and-run tactics to disrupt the flow of enemy troops and supplies and to inflict as much damage as possible. The site of action was a small fiberglass boat, and the dominant weapon was the Browning .50-caliber HB-M2 machine gun. Bryant belonged to one of the better-known operations of the Vietnam Brown Water Navy, Task Force 116 (Operation GAME WARDEN), the River Patrol Force. Activated in December, 1965, Task Force 116 underwent several permutations, being enlarged in 1968--the year that Bryant arrived in Vietnam--to four task groups assigned to specific rivers (Rottman, 5). The first Game Warden PBRs were operational in Spring, 1966; the boats were based on the Long Tau ship channel, Nha Be and at Cat Lo, near Vung Tau. (The Long Tau channel connects three rivers: the Saigon, the Nha Be and the Long Tau.) Speaking of the PBR, the most frequently observed patrol craft in the Mekong Delta, Alan L. "Buz" Lowe observes: "The PBR came to symbolize the Brown Water Navy in Vietnam. When the US Navy decided to commit river patrol forces, it found itself in need of a small, fast vessel that could maneuver in tight places. The Navy decided to use a 31-foot craft capable of 28 knots. The boat's armament consisted of a twin .50 caliber-machinegun turret in the bow, a single .50 caliber machine gun in the stern, and an M-60 machine gun and a Mark 18 40mm grenade launcher mounted amidships. Because its armor was limited, speed and armament became the PBR's best hope for protection. The PBR was born in an atmosphere of urgency and tested under actual combat conditions..." (12). Task Force 116 reached a peak strength of 258 craft, supported by aircraft and helicopters. Rottman makes the point that, "of the fourteen Medals of Honor awarded to Navy personnel in the Vietnam War, three were awarded to two PBR crewmen, one posthumously, and a river assault officer" (5). This was a task force of heroes.

Jimmy Bryant and men like him would not want to be put on a pedestal, however. "Salty," Rottman says, "is perhaps the best word to describe America's brown water sailors. Serving long days aboard small craft with few comfort amenities, distant from desk-bound officers, they viewed themselves as free-wheeling and independent from the spit and polish of the 'big ship Navy'" (16). Some wore Vietnamese black pajamas, the same as their Vietnamese crewmen. Warriors who didn't stand on ceremony--these were the seamen of the Brown Water Navy. They inhabited a world of mobile bases, patrolling, speed, searching out the enemy, and lightning-reaction ingenuity. The man who adapted and improvised, lived to tell his story.

Tom Hain explains on his informative web page, up since 1996, "The Mobile Riverine Force" (www.vietvet.org/hain.htm), that "the tactics we used were developed on the job," because there hadn't been a need for a force like the MRF since the Civil War. The degree of cooperation between Army and Navy also recalls Civil War times. In Hain's view, the terrain of combat was decisive. The Vietnam delta, he reminds us, "was laced with waterways, natural and man made. You couldn't dig a hole more than 2 feet deep without hitting water. The bad guys used the waterways too." On these dangerous waterways Jimmy Bryant operated, and every inch of brown water, or so it would appear, turned into a kill zone.

The Riverine forces, the subject of. Commander Don Sheppard's best-selling book, *Riverine: A Brown-Water Sailor In The Delta, 1967* (1992), took the fight to the enemy under the motto "Close and Kill." The men who fought the so-called River War, volunteers from the fleet, relied on strategy and teamwork. Each operation required an orchestration of various units, both water and ground; air support figured in, as well.

The task of the mobile riverine operation was tactical, rewarding daring, speed, and the surprise of the night ambush. Each four-man crew faced the danger of sorties into unknown territory, as the fragile boats navigated the muddy, unpredictable rivers. They accepted a tight living space that was damp, dusty and noisy; there was precious little privacy. Weather was always a factor, sometimes a major inhibiting factor. (It is estimated that weather, for example, monsoon rains, restricted PBR operations up to half of the time, especially early in the River War.) As the men of Game Warden hot-rodded down the brown water on diesel engines, the crewmen tried to forget that their vulnerable boats had little armor and that they might have to engage the enemy at distances of one yard or less. (Given the extremely close presence of the enemy, some PBR sailors received sniper training by the US Army.) For survival the brown water sailors counted on speed, firepower, tactical mobility--and each other.

Every PBR sailor had to overcome fear, for instance, that a patrolling craft would come under attack, catch fire and burn on the brown water. Fire meant beaching the boat and possible capture by the enemy. Bryant makes the point that, although his brown-water sailors were apprehensive about what night patrols might bring, since open contact with the enemy forces was more likely to occur at night, he detected no fear in either of his boat crews. Recognizing that his first responsibility was to keep his men alive, Bryant spent much time familiarizing his boat crews with the coming mission. "They all knew," he tells me in private correspondence, "a foolish move could cost us dearly. So everyone kept his head and dealt with everything as it came. Every new crew member was tutored until his confidence was what he-- and we--wanted it to be." Patrol Chief Bryant was guided by a simple code: "Don't let your guard down, or you might die." This outlook, and approach to naval operations, he instilled in his boat crews. They learned to be cautious and to trust one another. "When we were on patrol during the day on the Long Tao River searching sampans, junks and water taxis," Bryant says, "we always had two men covering the man searching for contraband, weapons and suspected VC. Our emotions were: 'Don't trust anyone, and be ready to respond if our boat crews are threatened.' " Trust was re-served for those fellow men who, in Bryant's words, "hit the Viet Cong and NVA Army as hard as they could and kept the boats afloat to live and fight another day."

Brown water warfare dates, of course, to the earliest times. Eight centuries before Christ the Egyptians developed the trireme, which sailed from the Nile River to the Mediter-ranean Sea. Lt. Col. Victor Croizat reminds the reader that the history of the United States, itself, is "rich in examples of naval operations complementing those of land armies, par-ticularly by forces operating on the rivers and lakes of the continent" (*Brown Water Navy*, 13). Beginning with the War of Independence, he continues, "brown water warfare has been a regular feature in early American military history" (13). The War of 1812, the Seminole Wars in Florida, the Mexican War--all included naval support operations on riv-ers. In 1846, for the Mexican conflict, the US Navy organized a naval brigade of ten ships, numerous boats, and 2500 men. But the most prominent use of naval river forces is in the

Civil War. "The importance of naval operations during the war," Croizat concludes, "becomes readily apparent on a map, where the Confederacy is seen to have consisted largely of a coastal plain and piedmont. The navy's blockade of the coast and its penetration of the Mississippi River basin thus helped to isolate the Confederacy and at the same time brought the navy into position to support the Union Army directly" (15). Using the blockade as a weapon, the Federal Navy played a critical role in the plan to divide and conquer the South. River operations figured prominently in the Union strategy, for instance, at Fort Henry in 1862, when ironclads contributed to General U.S. Grant's victory.

In 1967, relatively early in the Vietnam War (near the time of the Glassboro Summit), American journalists readily recognized that fierce river firefights on the rivers of Southeast Asia justified comparisons with Civil War river operations. In making this new "River War" understandable to a popular American audience, *Newsweek* didn't link brown river naval participation in Vietnam to the early western theatre of the Civil War, however, which was centered in Cairo, Illinois; instead, the magazine issue of 3 July 1967 looked to the American South: "Not since the Mississippi flotilla was deployed to fight the Civil War battles of Vicksburg and Shiloh, had the US Army found use for an assault force designed especially for river warfare. ...Last week [June, 1967] a US river-borne assault force went on the attack in the Mekong Delta, its most important vehicle an unwieldy-looking craft that bears a striking resemblance to the ironclads of a century ago. The force was called 'River Assault Flotilla One,' and its overall mission was to root out the Viet Cong from the river and swampland south of Saigon" (33). It was not only the media that drew the connection between Riverine operations and the Civil War. The brown water sailors, themselves, active on canals and rivers, chose the name "Monitor" for a Riverine vessel that had an army tank turret mounted on the front of it. Best known for its naval duel with the *Merrimac* in 1862, the Union *Monitor*--after the Latin MONERE, "to warn, advise"--became the generic term for shallow-draught vessels mounting large guns and ready to bombard the enemy from its ironclad abode. In the Brown Water Navy, the monitors searched riverbanks for fleeing VC in support of landing forces, escorted Armored Troop Carriers (ATCs), and covered the rear on riverine missions.

The final sentence of the 1967 *Newsweek* article articulates well the mission of the Brown Water Navy: "to root out the Viet Cong, etc." Besides removing entrenched enemy positions, the river patrol forces interdicted troops, weapons, and other shipments on water--from Vietnam and bordering countries--while providing protection for friendly shipping into South Vietnamese ports. "Buz" Lowe gives a thorough listing of the goals of Task Force 116, Game Warden: "...To enforce curfews, interdict VC infiltration, prevent taxation of water traffic by the Viet Cong and counter enemy movement and resupply efforts. In addition, the new force was to keep open the main shipping channel into Saigon by patrolling and minesweeping the Long Tau River" (12). Refining the description of the method and mission of the Game Warden patrols, Lt. Commander Thomas J. Cutler remarks in his classic book *Brown Water, Black Berets: Coastal and Riverine Warfare in Vietnam* (1988): "Stopping and searching suspicious craft was not the only mission... They often participated in nighttime ambushes, set up as a result of intelligence information or on the judgment of the patrol officer. PBRs concealed themselves along a riverbank and waited for expected enemy movement through the area, or shut down their engines and drifted silently through a suspect area using starlight scopes to detect enemy movements" (166-7).

Just as interesting to us are the perceptions of Chief Petty Officer Jimmy Bryant himself, who characterized his mission in these words:

> The River Wars in Vietnam consisted of operations designed to interdict the flow of men and materials to enemy forces trying to destroy the government in Saigon and to install their own. The US Navy was assigned to patrol the many Vietnamese rivers in small

boats able to travel the waterways at high speeds. Using hit-and-run tactics, brown water sailors disrupted the flow of troops and supplies, and inflict as much damage as possible on the enemy. I was assigned to the PBRs as patrol officer in charge of two river patrols boats that patrolled the rivers of South Vietnam in search of the enemy--and often found him.

Bryant arrived in Vietnam in fall 1968, a decisive year for the war and for the United States. He was part of the wave of American troops which would peak in Spring of 1969 at almost 550,000. Among those arriving in the same month, October, 1968, was Byron E. Holley, M.D., who recorded his experiences in the book, *Vietnam 1968-1969. A Battalion Surgeon's Journal* (1993). Holley describes the landing:

> As our World Airways Boeing 707 approached the coast of South Vietnam, the captain turned out all the interior lights as well as the navigation lights. He announced over the loudspeaker that, although they had never lost an airliner over Vietnam, he did not want to risk breaking a good record, so that all lights would remain extinguished until we were safely on the ground at Bien Hoa. It was a clear night, and every few minutes we could see brilliant flashes of light from exploding artillery shells somewhere off in the distance. It was beautiful in an eerie and silent sort of way--but served as a grim reminder of the unhealthy climate of our destination (17).

In this "unhealthy climate" Bryant landed, as he reports below. He arrived in a Saigon that was experiencing edgy, post-Tet days. In autumn, 1968 Saigon lay uneasily, ringed by VC-NVA dominated territory. To the southwest of Saigon stretched the Mekong River, its tributaries and delta now significantly under the red flag. Heavy concentrations of the enemy were south and southwest of a capital city still nervous about the fighting during the Tet Offensive of the past winter. No matter that the significance of Tet was mainly psychological. Never again could American or ARVN troops feel safe in the city, now suddenly vulnerable. Two major battles had been fought in Saigon in the year of Bryant's arrival, the second coming in spring when Communist mortar crews attacked the city. Clark Dougan, et al., in the book, *The Vietnam Experience. Nineteen Sixty-Eight* (1983), speak of the "Second Battle of Saigon" in 1968 after Tet (154ff.). Saigon, teeming with desperate refugees, had become a place of disillusionment and fear. 1968 had not been good for the nerves of the ancient city, founded on a Khmer site.

1968, in fact, had been just as bad for the United States. America was plainly going mad in a year that has brought forth no less that three scholarly, analytical books, the most recent of which is very recent, indeed: Jules Witcover's *The Year The Dream Died: Revisiting 1968 in America* (1997). It is difficult for historians to find a single adjective for the year 1968--the most frequent choices are "pivotal," "tumultuous," "depressing," "passionate," "dramatic," and "insane." Nor is it easy to recount, or even to absorb, the events and personalities of that single year: the Tet Offensive, Eugene McCarthy, Lyndon Johnson (and his resignation), the assassination of Dr. Martin Luther King, Jr. and Robert Kennedy, urban Civil Rights riots, H. Rap Brown, George Wallace, Spiro Agnew, the Democratic National Convention, the Paris peace talks, and the election of Richard Nixon.

Whatever the news of the hour in 1968 -- and who could keep up?--Vietnam was always in the background, coming home in living color every night on the TV set. It was plainly the lead story in the media. In search of a metaphor for the Vietnam War, Marshall Smelser and Joan R. Gundersen choose this unpleasant one: "The war in Vietnam pervaded life like a spreading stain" (*American History at a Glance*. 1978:253). Professor Lucas Powe, Jr., in reviewing Charles Kaiser's comprehensive book, *1968 In America. Music, Politics, Chaos, Counterculture, and the Shaping of a Generation* (1988), has this to say about the American perception of the Vietnam War in 1968:

The February Tet Offensive was an amazing catalyst. Gone was the belief in the light at the end of the tunnel and, finally, gone was the [television] network support of the war, so consistent for the previous three years. When a photographer could capture the national police chief shooting his pistol at point-blank range into the head of a Vietcong prisoner, the dissonance of the fight for freedom in the South was brought home. Walter Cronkite, whose stature grew as Johnson's tumbled, announced on his newscast that he was going to Vietnam again. This time, however, there was none of the flag waving boosterism of his 1965 trip. He returned home to do an hour-long television special concluding the war could not be won and America must negotiate an end to our involvement. (Quoted from the "publishing blurb" of 1/89 for the History Book Club)

During this time of defeatism and despair, of eroding civilian moral and global chaos in the year 1968, Jimmy Bryant went to Vietnam. His memoir tells of the situation that he found, which he has collected into almost fifty sections I would label "vignettes." Bryant experiences firefights, night operations, ambush, water mines, a helicopter ride, dangerous reptiles, South Vietnamese peasants, snipers, Navy Seal support, artillery fire, swamps, the death of comrades, civilian casualties, a VC interrogation, and debilitating personal injury. The clear impression, upon reading this book, is that the author is a reliable, brave and modest patriot who risked his life many times for his country and for his boat crews. In laconic prose, using a straightforward, annalistic technique that strives for an almost photographic accuracy, he speaks of life, death and patriotism. There is no hint in his account of the anti-values of the cynical 1990s, where patriotism can mean flag-waving and extremism. When Bryant speaks of liberty and heroism, he does so without a trace of irony. His words are therefore bracing and refreshing, taking us to a perhaps better time when duty, honor and country were more than empty rhetoric. Jimmy Bryant, a decent man who was greatly troubled by civilian entanglement in the Vietnam

War, spent one of the most turbulent times in postwar America, not avoiding his duty, but in doing it.

It is impossible to read Jimmy Bryant's memoir without being grateful that the United States has produced such men. May his chronicle contribute both to the intensive re-evaluation of the Vietnam War that we are witnessing and to the long-overdue national appreciation for men of his kind and character! Every book of this type is a concrete gesture that helps to counter, and even ameliorate, the shameful treatment many returning Vietnam veterans were forced to experience. Let it be emblazoned on whatever stone will last forever, making the words impossible to eradicate: Almost 60,000 Americans died in the Vietnam War; many thousands were wounded; and some are still missing. To those, like Jimmy R. Bryant, who fought bravely and who returned, we pledge never to forget their sacrifice. As the ancient Romans said: *Gratias Tibi Ago.*

Thank you.

PROLOGUE
Sometime in 1969

I arrived at our chief's quarters after a hard night on the river. A very hard night on the Vam Co Dong River, at Ben Luc. With a start I realized how close we had come to getting killed. A bullet had taken a chunk out of my ear, and one my men on my cover boat had gotten hurt. In the dark hutch I broke out a bottle of whiskey that I kept in my locker for just such occasions and poured a glass to calm my nerves. I thought of events of the day while sitting alone in the dark, just me, a table in the middle of the room, a bottle, a glass, and the darkness. How and when did I get here, anyway?

Map 1

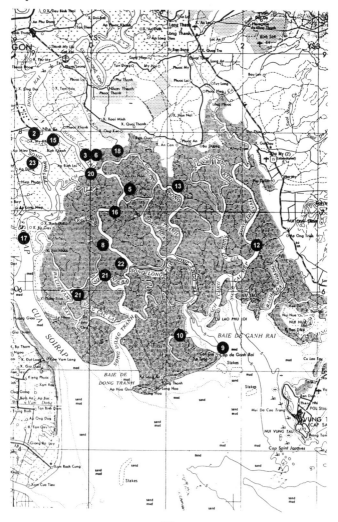

28

Chapter 1
Landing in Saigon

1 October 1968. The pilot's voice came over the speaker: "Buckle up gentlemen, we'll be landing in Saigon in a few minutes. We're currently at 30,000 feet and will be going down pretty fast from this altitude in hopes of not drawing any ground fire. Best of luck to you on your tour here."

What a landing! It was almost as if we had fallen from the sky. A strong case of white knuckles showed on all of us as we came down fast, swallowing hard to keep our stomachs down, and ears popping with the pressure change. It was already dark, around 21:30, when the plane touched down.

We had landed at the Tan Son Nhut air base in Saigon. After retrieving our seabags and personal gear, we were greeted by two navy personnel who "welcomed" us to Vietnam. One told us to get a move on. A bus was waiting to take us to one of Saigon's finest hotels. I was surprised to see sailors wearing flak jackets and side arms. One was carrying an M-16 as he rode shotgun. We were driven to a high-rise hotel of about five stories and were led to a briefing room. The Chief in charge said we would be staying in the hotel a few days until we could be sent to our assigned units. "Make yourselves comfortable," he urged us. "But don't hang around open windows too much, a sniper may take a shot at you." How comforting! A quick check revealed that the windows had heavy screens on them. As we would soon learn, the screens were there to prevent grenades from being thrown in on us.

My first geography lesson. In Saigon windows weren't for looking out; they were for bullets and grenades.

After being assigned bunks and "dismissed," I thought maybe that a shower would do me good. Other newcomers agreed with me. Looking around, I asked where one could be found. A seaman said he would show us, so we followed him. We entered a room with a spigot, bucket, galvanized wash tub and a floor drain. That was it. This was hardly the Ritz.

"Enjoy your shower guys! Oh, by the way, no hot water here either, and the water also runs very slow, he added as he left."

Next day, all of us navy newcomers to Vietnam were issued a side arm and ammo. Our choices were the .45 automatic or the .38 revolver. Since I liked the automatic better, I chose it and was issued four full clips with my weapon.

Four of us decided to leave the hotel for awhile to look the capital city over. We weren't too impressed with what we saw. There was a smell about the area, an odor that wasn't very pleasant. On the crowded streets it seemed like every person was trying to hustle every other person. Dope-- marijuana I suppose--was offered us by one of the Vietnamese who spoke English pretty well. We refused his offer, however. In a few of the small, crowded shops we talked to some of the other GIs we ran into. We soon learned that most of them didn't want to be there. On our way back to the hotel we were propositioned by some of the local ladies of the night; again we refused. One of the chiefs with us observed, "Just imagine what kind of diseases you could catch from them!"

After three days of living in a hotel that had been converted into a barracks, eating nothing but C-rations, and washing in cold water, we were ready to go to our assigned units.

Our transportation assignment arrived and roll call took place. We learned we would be leaving shortly for Nha Be, southeast of Saigon, where several River Patrol Divisions were located. My assignment was to River Division 591. As we gathered our gear, another briefing was called.

"Guys," the driver said, "we are going on a bus to Nha Be, which is about thirty-odd miles from here. We may encounter sniper fire or be outright attacked. But we will not stop for any reason. We will be going pretty fast over these rough roads. Keep your heads down if we are fired upon. An armed escort will lead the way for us. So, wish us luck! We'll need it."

The bus ride was uneventful. We could tell the driver was nervous, however, because the bus had a number of fresh bullet holes taken on some previous trip. Delivered safely to Nha Be, we expressed gratitude to the driver.

Chapter 2
Nha Be

In the morning we received another briefing, this one to assign us quarters and to inform us about our new home-- the base. The Seabees had used bottom sand pumped out of the Dong Nai River to build the whole military compound, extending out from the small town of Nha Be. Nha Be was one of the original bases for river patrol boats on the delta and the Rung Sat in the mid-60s; the other was Cat Lo. I was assigned to Chief's quarters, a tin-covered building with loads of sandbags around it. The rooms were merely partitions, set up on each side of a hallway in one long building-- our "home" for awhile. I got settled in and met some of the other Chiefs and First Class Petty Officers I would be working with.

Several of us found the mess hall and had the first good hot meal since leaving the States. The steak was probably the best I'd had in over a year. But steak was not the only treat. We received our first malaria pills, a weekly requirement while in Vietnam.

That night, when everything seemed quiet, I walked out to the river's edge. Looking out into the distance to the northeast, I could see dozens of night illumination shells, continuously bursting in the air, and I could make out distant gunfire. I wondered if my wife had made it safely back home to our children in Virginia Beach since we had had to part in San Diego. As I stood by the river, my mind seemed flooded with thoughts. Out in the dark river was an old cargo ship that had been sunk by a water-mine. A large part of the wreck was still showing above the surface of the river. Tracer fire from automatic weapons lit the sky about three miles away; it looked like a pretty heavy firefight. Suddenly the Seawolf helicopter gun ships went airborne in that direction. From my vantage point, their strike with rockets and mini-guns was serious--and severe. So this is what being in the River Patrol Force is all about, I told myself. Tomorrow I guess I'll know first hand.

All of us newcomers were directed to the briefing room to meet our skipper and executive officer. We were welcomed to Nha Be as participants in an operation called Game Warden. Game Warden, which would soon make the history books, had started with "MacLeod's Navy," the legendary group under Lt. Kenneth L. MacLeod III, USN. His two converted LCPLs in 1965 were the first boats to patrol the rivers under our flag. The initial Game Warden PBRs had arrived in March 1966. The Riverine task groups expanded in 1968, an important year for Game Warden, Task Force 116, the River Patrol Force.

In the briefing room we were introduced all around and informed of our duties and responsibilities. Each of us was paired with a seasoned vet who had been on the river for a time and had experienced a few firefights. I was linked up with Howard Maner, SM1 [signalman first class] who had been in country awhile and had seen a good bit of action with his PBRs. He was patrol officer in charge of two river patrol boats with crews of four or five on each boat. The boats had twin .50 cal. machine guns in the forward gun turret, a single .50 cal. On the back by the stern, an M60 mounted on the starboard side about midship, and a Honeywell M79 semi-automatic grenade launcher mounted on the port side. In the gun locker were a few M16 rifles, several types of grenades, and a pair of hand-held M79 grenade launchers. All of this firepower floated on a fiberglass hull propelled by two 250-horsepower diesel engines, pushing water through Jacuzzi pumps.

With that entire engine horsepower, these boats could get up and scat. However, there was just one little problem. Little armor. Because of the lightweight fiberglass construction, a bullet would easily pass through the boat.

To get me ready for action, Maner took me out on a few day patrols and one night patrol. We searched several sampans on the day patrols and detained two suspected Viet

Cong, taking them to the South Vietnamese compound for interrogation. My records show I found nothing else worth reporting. The night patrol was also uneventful. During all the hours of darkness, curfew was in effect on the river. Therefore, anyone on water invited capture or attack.

I got my own patrol from the division commander after having spent a few days on the river familiarizing myself with all the boat equipment and some of the areas of patrol. He made me patrol officer in charge of boats numbered "19" and "72," and gave me a call sign: "Guilt X-ray Hotel." My cover boat would be "Hotel One." My first boat captains were Engineman First Class Robert P. Stark and Signalman First Class R.L. Nemmers. Both were very capable men with good reputations on the river. Before getting night assignments, we ran a few day patrols. From my fellow brown-river sailors I learned about the risk of capture. The Vietcong had put out rewards of $2000 American money for patrol officers and $1000 American for boat captains.

Chapter 3
Firefight at the Hanging Tree

Prior to every patrol, the tactical operations duty officer briefed the patrol commanders and boat captains. He informed us what was known to be going on in the areas we were to patrol, and he told us about any special operations by other friendly forces, as well as about intelligence reports on enemy activity. From the briefing we learned that not much was expected tonight in our area. About two miles to the north, several VC had been sighted. The Officer told us sharply, "Be aware and stay alert!"

We left the base about an hour before dark for our turn on the river. Our boats were assigned the patrol just south of the base. After making a complete run of our patrol area and checking a few sampans scurrying to get back home before the night and the curfew came, we drifted in the current, vigilantly watching the banks. About 09:30 or so, I suggested to my boat captains that we should check the area around the Hanging Tree. (Most places where a significant action had taken place had acquired a name.) A small stream fed the river at that spot. As we slowly approached the area, moving maybe five or six knots, I tried to pop a flare over the area. But it didn't want to work. So I removed my .45 and bumped the base of the flare with the side of it; this time it ignited and illuminated the area.

Our cover boat followed about forty to fifty feet behind us--all of us travelling about sixty feet from the bank. Stark, my Boat Captain ignited a second flare. We couldn't see anything for a few seconds, but then all hell broke loose, just as the light from the flares began to illuminate the area. The bow of my boat took a strong rocket hit. The exploding rocket knocked my bow gunner unconscious, filling his legs with shrapnel and bursting his eardrums. The concussion stunned EN1 Stark and me and knocked both of us to the deck in the rear of the boat just as a heavy salvo of automatic weapons fire peppered our craft. Recovering quickly, Stark got to the rear .50cal. deck gun and began returning heavy fire. Our cover boat, skippered by SM1 Nemmers, was also receiving fire from the bank. When he saw what was happening, his boat began returning fire with all his crew had.

Still stunned, I managed to get back to the radio to call for helicopter gunship support. I got to the coxswain station, reached over, slapped the throttles forward to the pegs, and yelled, "Let's get out of here!" Since our coxswain was not yet recovered from the blast, I took the wheel with my left hand and aimed us toward the middle of the river. Our cover boat followed suit. We were putting down a wall of fire as we cleared the area to the east. My communication to base through the sound of gunfire was, "Moon River, this is X-ray Hotel; we are under attack from rockets and heavy automatic weapons' fire from the Hanging Tree. Request Seawolf support. Looks like three or four rockets fired and it looks like ten to fifteen small arms positions. We have wounded men."

The answer came back, Roger, standby.

At that moment another voice came on the radio, "X-ray Hotel, we are underway to your location, repeat number of firing positions, their location, and are you clear, over?"

"Roger, we are clearing to the east. There are ten to fifteen firing positions coming from the east side of the small stream on the north side of the main river."

"Roger," the Seawolves came back, "say when you are clear."

We had moved about 500 yards by this time and had ceased firing. "We are clear." The two Seawolves arrived at the firing zone within two minutes, put in about ten to fifteen rockets and strafed the area with mini-guns. Both gun ships saturated the area with fire. Upon completion of their strike, they remained in the area because, in order to take our wounded man back to the base for medical help, we had to pass back by the ambush site.

A strong smell of burned cordite hung heavily in the air, and its smoke was visible to all of us. Both boats put down a wall of fire with our .50s and M60s as we passed back through the "hell zone."

After the firing run and we were clear, both boats returned at top speed to Nha Be. There we informed our tactical operation center of the extent of our injuries. An ambulance was to be at the pier when we arrived with battle casualties.

Considering all the weapons fired at us from such close range, we were very fortunate that only four men had been hurt. My forward gunnersmate had severe shrapnel wounds in his legs, and his eardrums had burst and were bleeding from the explosion in the bow of the boat. But he was alive, and that is what mattered most to me. Three others were slightly wounded, small shrapnel wounds and concussions--but otherwise O.K.

After delivering our wounded to the medical personnel waiting for us at the pier, we went in for military debriefing. Boy, the adrenaline was really flowing in both boat crews! They acted as though they were indestructible and could go out and win the war tonight. I knew they were most vulnerable when experiencing this kind of high, so the command duty officer supported me my saying, That's enough for tonight guys, we still have tomorrow.

[Editor's Note: EN3 L.J. Kramer, a participant in the just-described patrol action wrote the following words on the conduct of Jimmy Bryant:

9 Jan. '69 Chief Bryant. While on routine patrol on the Long Tau river our PBR came under heavy rocket and machine gun fire after the Chief popped a flare to check possible enemy positions. The Chief was knocked down on the engine covers but got up again, directing our fire as he headed for the radios. Due to his calmness under fire he was able to tell the Seawolf helicopters exactly where we were, enabling them to arrive almost immediately, as we left the kill zone. His quick actions were a determining factor in our getting out of the kill zone.]

Chapter 4
Chief Sampan Smith

I knew a brown water sailor whom some called reckless. One thing was certain: his desire for action was unmatched. "Sampan" Smith, a chief and patrol officer in one of the other river divisions operating with us, had been "in country" quite some time, maybe a year or so. He had the reputation on the river as one of the most aggressive patrol officers in seeking out and destroying the enemy. Chief Smith would take his patrols out at night, making himself and his crews intentional targets of attack. When the onslaught came, his crews would return fire, overwhelming the attackers, killing or capturing them.

Smith's patrols were able to recover lots of documents and weapons. Sampans were his biggest targets, which earned him the nickname "Sampan" Smith. His boat captain said Smith would not wear a flak jacket or helmet while on patrol. Once he had arrived in his desired or assigned area of patrol, Sampan Smith would break out his folding lawn chair and sit on the back of the boat in the middle of the river, drifting, no lights on in total silence in the darkness. Then he would light up a cigarette, which quite often became an irresistible target for the Viet Cong. This tactic worked for him several times, but last night was not one of them, at least not in his favor.

Automatic weapons' fire and B-40 rockets hit the boat he was riding in. Two or three rockets penetrated his vessel, as did many bullets, leaving holes too numerous to count. One rocket hit him in the head, killing him and two others, while leaving two additional men seriously wounded. I wasn't able to tell how many casualties their cover boat had taken. I do know that the cover boat captain called in the Seawolves for protection and radioed medivac to care for the wounded. Having seen the boat that was recovered after the fight, it's hard to believe anyone could have lived through that. A very sobering sight, with a lesson on how dangerous it is out on these rivers.

Chapter 5
Water Mine

One morning at briefing before day patrol, we learned shipping was coming up the river toward Saigon from the gulf. We were to escort the vessel through each of our assigned patrol areas and drop it off for the next patrol to escort past Nha Be.

Drifting in the lower area of our assigned patrol zone on the Long Tau, we were informed by radio that one cargo ship had started up the river. We scanned the area with lookouts and binoculars. The river edges had been defoliated with Agent Orange. Not much greenery had survived, so we could see a few hundred feet back from the water in most places--if the banks were low enough, and the majority was when the tide was in. Most ships tried to use the high tides for their transit up river because it put more water under the hull and allowed them to avoid the six- to eight- knot speed of the current when the tide was going out.

Our boats drifted down into a curve in the river and sighted the ship south of us. It was moving at a pretty good speed, maybe twelve to fifteen knots. We got out of the curve and started our escort north, leading the ship maybe 300 yards. As I looked back to see the ship enter the curve we had occupied a few minutes earlier, I saw a tremendous explosion about thirty to fifty feet to the starboard side of the ship. A very near miss for what we think was a 500-pound remote controlled VC water mine. Seconds earlier our two PBRs and their crews rode directly over it.

At top speed we returned to check things out. I sent the cover boat on ahead of the ship to continue the escort. The ship we were assigned to protect was thankfully undamaged. It continued on its way, but I'm confident at a faster speed.

With .50 caliber machine gun fire and with M-79 grenades, we raked the north bank of the river back in a tree line about 200 yards from the curve in which the explosion had occurred. We set one fire back there and heard a strong secondary explosion. After the firing, our boat fell in behind the ship and covered its stern on up past Nha Be. There rested a largely submerged, rusting cargo ship, the *Baton Rouge Victory*, which had been sunk. After our little adventure with the enemy mine, we fully realized what a serious threat it presented to all of us. What could have been a disaster, thus turned out to be a timely--and very useful--warning.

Thereafter we returned to our regular patrol, checking sampans and junks that came through our area. We were looking for contraband, weapons, and ID cards of suspected Viet Cong hiding among the people. That day the South Vietnamese authorities at Nha Be received three suspects from us whom we had detained on the river.

Chapter 6
Another Water Mine, with Disastrous Results

Shortly after the attempted mining of the ship we had escorted, Boatswain Mate Chief Everett Collier was on late evening patrol near Hanging Tree, where we had had previous contact. His patrol sighted a couple of sampans back in the small stream leading into the river. Collier let the first sampan pass, but opened fire on the second when he found five VC aboard. After the fight settled down, but before it ended, our crew found a mine, which was to cost several lives.

Here follows the official record of this firefight, written by Chief Collier:

171941H Jan.
Boats 23/24
BMC Collier, Pat. Off.

Supported PRU element that made contact with two sampans at XS997787. They let the first pass and took the second with five VC aboard under fire and called for extraction. PBRs proceeded to extract and took one sampan with two VC aboard under fire and found an object approx. 6' X 18" which was later identified as a mine. PBRs extracted and reinserted PRUs, returned to Nha Be and picked up EOD and more PRUs. PBRs then returned to area with air cover and towed mine to Nha Be where EOD attempted to disarm it and it exploded. Results seven VC BC [five by PRUs, two by PBR] three personnel from the division suffered broken eardrums from mine explosion and sent to CONUS.

When the mine exploded, shrapnel from it seriously

wounded several of the men who were watching it being disarmed. The explosion killed the Explosive Ordinance Disposal team that was trying to disarm it and seriously wounded several of the spectators interested in seeing what was going on. The total number of casualties would have been covered in a separate report not distributed to, or made available to, patrol officers.

Chapter 7
A Wild Helicopter Ride
and the Blocking Force

Night patrol. This one would lead us to an unfamiliar location, on one of the narrow back streams off the Soi Rap River. Although the charts gave us accurate geographical information, we needed to see a way out if we got into trouble. Therefore we requested an aerial view of our destination. My boat captains and I climbed into a helicopter with a hotshot army warrant officer pilot who looked all of nineteen years old. We looked at each other, silently asking, Should we do this? Within seconds we were airborne and flying over the river about fifteen feet off the water. As we turned to leave the main river, the nipa palm growing along the banks slapped the bottom of the helicopter! Not exactly recommended for helicopter school--and quite a hair raising ride. But we survived it. I asked the pilot why he had a couple of flack jackets under his feet and seat. He responded with, "I don't wanna get shot in the butt, that would be hard to take." Upon returning to the base, we thanked him for the ride.

We can joke about it now, after almost thirty years, but I want my feelings to be clear. Support personnel like the young warrant officer, Seawolf gunship pilots, gun crews, and all others have my sincere respect for having helped the River Patrol Force do its job.

After viewing our prospective patrol from the air, we decided it was not a good idea to go into that area at night. The streams were too narrow and too close to one of the villages. If we had to fight our way out, we reasoned, our fire could kill some of the innocent villagers.

Instead, we were assigned the lower leg of the Long Tao, where Charlie was often spotted and where patrols were easy nighttime targets. After arriving on station and surveying our patrol area, both our boats began drifting in the river current with only one engine on. Idling like this held down the engine noise, while allowing us to maintain headway for control in an emergency. All nine of our crewmembers were on watch, searching the banks for movement. The night came on us rather quickly; or so it seemed. No stars were showing in the dark sky, and the wind was calm. We had not observed any hostile activity up to this point. But about 21:30 our radio came alive.

"X-ray Delta, X-ray Hotel, X-ray Foxtrot, this is Moon River, standby to copy, over." Each of our patrols acknowledged the call. Standing by our plastic covered chart to copy down the message, I found our grease pencil and flashlight. It was a long, collective coded message, meant for my unit and two other patrols on the Long Tao. Immediately we all acknowledged receipt of it. When broken down from our codebook, the message instructed all three patrols to join forces at once and proceed to coordinates YS220650 in order to set up a night blocking force in support of American army forces.

Ltjg. A. C. Beck II was selected to be in charge of the six-boat blocking force. He contacted each of the other patrol officers, saying to rendezvous with him at YS010750. We acknowledged his call and proceeded up river to his location with throttles wide open. By the time our patrol arrived, the other two were drifting near the mouth of the Dong Tranh, where it forked off to the northeast of the Long Tao shipping channel.

"Hotel Foxtrot, this is Delta, come alongside, Hotel One, Foxtrot One, watch the banks, over," came the order from Mr. Beck.

We all acknowledged him. Maneuvering alongside, we tied a line to his boat; BMC Everett Collier secured his vessel on Beck's other side. We instructed our boat crews to keep a sharp eye out while we talked.

"Chief Collier, Chief Bryant, he said, the Army is in heavy contact with Charlie and the NVA over on the Cai

Mep. We have been assigned to set up a blocking force of six boats and provide river support as needed. We are to capture, or stop anyone, from escaping by way of the river. Also, we are to cover our forces' backs. If any boats cross the river, heading in the direction of the fighting, we stop them. We will enter the Dong Tranh here, so stay tight. Let's try to get there as fast as we can! If Charlie takes a shot at us on our way back there, return his fire, but keep on going. Stop only if forced to. Chief Bryant, your patrol will follow me; Chief Collier, your patrol will bring up the rear. Keep your eyes open, guys. Quickly tell your boat captains and crews what we are doing, cast off, and let's get moving!"

Our cover boat crews got the information quickly, and the six-boat convoy entered the Dong Tranh at full speed. The river narrowed as we proceeded deeper into the Forest of Assassins and on into the darkness. The PBRs were all kicking up white water rooster tails as we watched the banks for muzzle flashes or rocket trails. Our radar was working well, and all boats steered by radar at about thirty knots. Taking the curves and turns at high speed, everyone was tense and alert. After about half an hour the narrow streams began widening as we approached our assigned blockade area. After entering the Go Gia, we turned and headed north on the Cai Mep. Within a few minutes we could see gunfire, tracers, flares and explosions on the eastern side of the river.

"X-ray Hotel, X-ray Foxtrot: this is X-ray Delta. Take up positions about a half-click apart and maintain them unless otherwise directed, over," Ltjg. Beck commanded on the radio.

We acknowledged him, slowing our boats to a stop after we were in position to watch the river and the riverbanks. In the slow current we drifted approximately 200 yards from the east bank, listening and watching the radar for boat traffic. First we used the starlight scope, and next our binoculars, while our boat captains kept us close to our assigned positions. The air was calm, I remember thinking. "The sky is still overcast and it is, oh, so dark out here!"

The previous gunfire had abated, and all had seemed

quiet for a time. My boat captain moved us up a little closer to the bank upstream and cut the engines off again. Instantly we could hear American voices on the bank nearest to us. After a few minutes of sitting there, all hell broke loose on our army friends on shore. They received AK47 automatic weapon fire, followed by M16 automatic fire, followed by several hand grenade explosions. The sky was alight with tracer rounds. I told my boat crew, "Get your heads down, guys! We don't want to take any accidental hits."

The sounds of battle carried through the night across the water. I heard screaming voices, yelling, and long bursts of automatic weapons fire. "Medic, I'm hit!" "There he is!" This and the sounds of crying we were able to pick out of the night air. Then came the fresh smell of cordite smoke, drifting out across the surface of the river.

Frustrated that we were unable to help our comrades, we had to wait on the water. Our patrols could only cover their backs and follow instructions. About ten minutes after the firefight had erupted sounds of motorized vehicles came from north of where the fighting was going on. Still to be heard were loud voices and frequent bursts of M16s. All at once, night illumination shells lit up the sky over where the ground troops lay. The light carried out into and over the river. This glow allowed us to see clearly all the blocking forces. I instructed our boat captain to move us a little farther out into the river. The gunfire had ceased by the time that the motorized vehicles arrived. While the policing up was going on, all the commotion carried out to us on the water.

Meanwhile we maintained our stations, and finally the light from the last night illumination shell faded into darkness. Activity on the bank continued for about three hours; then all was quiet. After about an hour's quiet, our lead patrol officer suggested we drop anchor. We acknowledged him, but made sure we could get underway quickly, if we had to.

The hours dragged on, and we were all very tired. Slowly the light became visible in the eastern sky. At first light the curfew on the river lifts, and the village and river people start coming back out. When a few small fishing boats showed up, we knew it was time to go home. We were directed to pull up anchor, join forces with one another, and head back to Nha Be. Our trip home was without incident. Probably Charlie was tired and needed some sleep, too.

Chapter 8
Baby on Board?

Our assignment today took us about two miles from one of the tiny villages on the banks of the rivers we patrol. Some, like this one, contained small South Vietnamese army outposts and compounds. A call came in on my radio, "X-ray Hotel; this is Moon River [our tactical operation center]. Pick up medical emergency at the village in your area and deliver to home base, over."

"Moon River, this is X-ray Hotel." "Roger, on our way," was our response.

We pulled into the makeshift pier that was made from scrap lumber. Our cover boat kept an eye out for us, as we eased our way in and alongside. A South Vietnamese army soldier brought his wife out; she was in obvious pain, about to have a baby. We helped her onto the boat, spread out some foul weather jackets and ponchos on the engine covers and helped her to lie down. Her husband also came along. I told the boat captain, "Let's move it!"

Clearing the pier, we backed out into the main stream. The radio crackled "Moon River, X-ray Hotel. We've got the patient on board with her husband and are proceeding to your location. Request you have medical personnel standing by on the pier. Repeat, on the pier, over."

"Roger that," they came back.

As we pulled out into the river heading north, the woman began hollering with pain because her labor was very well advanced, indeed. I asked our engineer, "Can we get any more speed out of these boats?"

"Our throttles are pegged and the pumps are clean," he replied. "Let's just hope we make it."

We all thought we were about to deliver a baby. On the radio again, "Moon River, are the medical personnel at the pier yet? We will be there in ten minutes, over."

"Roger," they came back laughing at us; "the corpsmen will be there." Luckily our boats "got up in step," and we made good time.

Our approach to the pier was quite speedy, and as the boat bumped alongside, we had the soldier's wife up and onto a stretcher before the second line was tied up. The corpsmen put her into the waiting ambulance and drove away.

My boat captain turned to me and said, "Chief, I don't want to go through that again."

"Same here," we all agreed.

That evening when we came back in from patrol, the chief hospital corpsman who had picked up our mother-to-be at the pier came into the chief's lounge of our barracks and walked up to me. Smiling, he announced, "Thanks, you son of a bitch! Her water broke as we entered the door of sick bay and messed up the whole damn place."

I said, "You're welcome! How is she?"

He said, "She and her little girl are doing fine, but the father is a nervous wreck." Some things are universal, I guess.

Chapter 9
Shuttle Trip to Can Gio
with ARVN Troops

There was one assignment we didn't particularly like. Nevertheless, we had to perform it from time to time. Our instructions were to take about fifteen ARVN troops [Army, Republic of Vietnam] from Nha Be to Can Gio, a South Vietnamese outpost out near the gulf. A good long trip, so we topped off the fuel, loaded the soldiers up, and headed down river.

It seemed there was always a problem with ARVN soldiers. Sometimes they were caught stealing, and other times they messed around things in the boats they were supposed to leave alone. My boat contained half of the ARVN troops, while the cover boat had the other half. About a half-hour after our departure from Nha Be, at full speed on our way to Can Gio I became uncomfortable with them on board. Still, I continued our mission.

The water became quite choppy when we departed the river and started across the bay to the compound at Can Gio. Both boats tied up to the small pier and the soldiers disembarked, thanked us and waved good-by, as they walked away. I told both boat captains to check both boats thoroughly before we moved out, and they did. My gunnersmate found a hand grenade in the grenade locker with the pin pulled, toilet paper wrapped loosely around the bail and sitting up on end. Had we gone back out onto the choppy water, and had the grenade turned over in the grenade locker from the rocking of the boat, the bail would have popped and produced a major boom. A good booby trap from our supposedly friendly passengers, but this time it didn't work. The cover boat checked out O.K.

Chapter 10
Spotting a Destroyer's Artillery and a Snake in the Boat at Night

An American destroyer off the coast out beyond Can Gio was ready to use its big guns as artillery to saturate a known Viet Cong staging area about 22:00. The ship required a ground spotter to direct its fire. Our patrol received the destroyer's radio frequency and went to a location near the target area at the appointed time. Hoping that the VC wouldn't detect us until this mission was over, we positioned our boats about a half-mile from the target and dropped anchor in a swampy area about a mile off the main river channel. Our boats anchored about thirty feet apart. The destroyer established contact with us, we gave them our location, and they confirmed our knowledge of the target area. Within a couple of minutes the radio said, "Firing spotting round." A few seconds later the destroyer's white phosphorus round went off directly over the designated target.

My radio response to them was, "You are on target. Fire for effect!" Both of our boat crews saw what an American destroyer is capable of. It looked like a two-mile area was totally shredded from the rapid explosions. Several secondary explosions were also heard. After a short pause, the destroyer came back on the radio to ask for an evaluation. It was hard to describe, so I told them the target area was totally saturated, small fires were burning, and several secondary explosions were audible. They thanked us and we said "Good job! Sure glad you guys are on our side."

As we prepared to leave the area, our boat seaman pulled up anchor, while our boat engineer opened the Jacuzzi pump covers to clean out the debris we had picked up on the way. He yelled out, "Damn, a snake just bit me!" By moonlight we could briefly see the snake, now being slung over the side, as the bitten man attempted to get rid of it. The reptile was about three feet long, but we had no idea what kind it might be. Putting the pump covers back on quickly, we informed our cover boat captain and crew about the snake and the pending emergency.

"Let's go," I yelled over to our cover boat and picked up the radio hand set. "Moon River, this is X-ray Hotel, we have a man with snakebite. We're on our way to your location fast as we can. Please have emergency medical personnel standing by. Our other mission is complete, over."

"Roger, X-ray Hotel," was the reply.

Just in case the snake was poisonous, we put a tourniquet on the sailor's arm. This would at least prevent poison from moving too fast through. A few minutes later, we departed the swamp and entered the main river at full throttle, heading north.

"X-ray Hotel, medical personnel want to know if you kept the snake, over."

"Roger, negative, can't help you there. Our patient said he was glad to get rid of it before it bit him again, over," was my reply.

On the way home, we were concerned about a possible firefight, because there had been many previous attacks on our night patrols. Tonight would be especially hazardous, for under a clear sky and a full moon, we were clearly visible. Fortunately, during a tense forty-five minute ride, no one attacked us, and we made it home safely.

When we arrived at the pier, our patient was met by medical personnel and medivaced to Saigon by helicopter for evaluation. He was back within a week. It appears the snake was not poisonous after all. Upon his return, he checked in with us and said, "It's good to be back on the boats! A guy could get killed in Saigon. That place up there is a madhouse."

Chapter 11
Chief's Quarters

I was telling some of the other patrol commanders in our chief's lounge about the snake we had encountered. Chief McGowan from one of the other river divisions spoke up and said there sure were some mean snakes out there. One afternoon, he said, his patrol spotted a sampan drifting in the river. Suspecting a booby trap, he cautiously eased his boat up close to it and used his boat hook, which is about ten feet long, to lift the floor boards. Cautiously, he lifted one and a cobra over seven feet long came out, spitting venom and ready to strike. He backed off, then came back for a better look. McGowan figured out that someone had caught the cobra, pinched up some of its skin, nailed it to the bottom of the boat, and then put the floor boards back over him. I guess that was why the serpent was so mad. Mac said he backed off a distance and tossed a concussion grenade in on it, destroying the sampan with the snake. We had heard this same story in the States in Patrol Boat tactical school; it was good now to hear it from the source.

Chapter 12
Australian Encounter

During our morning briefing prior to going on patrol, the duty officer informed us that last night there had been heavy contact with the VC. One patrol unit spotted a junk with quite a few people on board. Illuminated by flares, the inhabitants were told to surrender. But they chose to fight instead, opening up on our patrols with automatic weapon fire. So our boats returned the fire. Twenty-one people were killed. Some were North Vietnamese soldiers in uniform and others were men, women and children. Several weapons and intelligence documents were recovered. But I couldn't get the women and children out of my mind. Each time I thought of the innocents, who were casualties of this war effort, I felt sick to my stomach.

We left the boat dock around 07:00 and headed out to our assigned area of patrol. This time the stream was quite wide because it was on the Go Gia and Cai Mep, out near the gulf. When I saw it, I thought of a large lake. My boat captain pointed out a striking absence of South Vietnamese fishing boats. As we cruised the area near the banks looking for any type of activity, we spotted two fast moving rubber boats sitting low in the water. I wasn't certain what we had, because they were some distance away. We loaded rounds into the gun chambers of the .50s and M60s and increased our speed to full throttle ahead. The boats also spotted us and headed our way at an equally fast pace. I made sure our flag was flying clear, just in case we had friendlies in the area are that we had not been informed of. As we closed on them and they on us, I said, "Hold your fire!" They don't look like Charlie. We came nearer to each other and slowed down with guns at the ready. As they came close, an old sergeant spoke up and said, "Mate, you almost got shot! A good thing we saw your flag. Aren't you Yanks a long way from home?"

We invited them alongside, they accepted, and their cover boat tied up next to ours. It turned out they were an Australian group which, unknown to us, was patrolling the northeast section of the Rung Sat Special Zone. Nor had they known about us. We shared information about some of the known VC staging areas and where contact had been made with the enemy. I informed the Aussies that we were in that place to monitor and report any activity. Also, we were to blow up any bunkers we could find near the river's edge.

It was nice to visit with these English-speakers. When we asked if there was anything we could do for them, the sergeant asked if we had any extra food. He would greatly appreciate some. Our crews broke out some C-rations and offered them to the Australians. Sarge said our chow was gourmet food, compared to what they had. So we gave them everything edible on board, except what we needed for the rest of the day. We shared some ten cases in all. Surprised and grateful, they wished us luck and Godspeed. Then we parted and resumed our patrols.

River traffic was noticeably light, with only a few fishermen out. That was a good indication enemy activity was nearby. We ran our boats near the banks on the southwest side close to a point where the Cai Mep and the Go Gia join. Three or four men ran away upon seeing us. Near them were several bunkers, so we put in seven or eight M-79 rounds, and our sharp-shooting gunners mates put a couple of LAW [long range anti-tank weapons] rounds into each bunker from each boat. I am not aware of any shots fired at us. Since the night patrols needed our boats for on-coming crews, we returned to the base in time for the boats to be serviced.

Chapter 13
Patrol Hit at Night

A few days later, my patrol was paired with Ltjg. Shannon's for a night operation into some very unfriendly back water streams. Our boats left the pier just after dark. A short while later we turned onto the Song Dong Tranh and then onto the Tac Ong Trun, a feeder river to the main shipping channel on our way. Our mission was to set up a four-boat bank-side ambush in a known staging area near where we had previously blown the bunkers on the Go Gia. My boats were third and fourth in the formation. Just as we went around a bend in the river, we came under attack from both banks: a crossfire. Two rockets hit us in the bow. One went through the boat near the water line and exploded outside as it hit the water. The other went all the way through the boat, passing between several grenades in the grenade locker and on out to explode near the VC firing positions on the south bank.

Numerous automatic weapons and rockets fired at us. All four of our boats returned fire to both banks with all we had. We directed most fire at the north firing positions because that seemed to be the origin of the rockets, and more. While clearing the kill zone to the east, I picked up the radio handset, still returning fire, yelling into it, "Moon River, X-ray Hotel with X-ray Delta, We are under attack from heavy automatic weapons and numerous rockets. Our location coordinates are Yankee Sierra 122741. Request air strike, over."

"Roger, X-ray Hotel, standby," was their reply.

We cleared the strike zone and ceased fire. Almost immediately a strange voice came on the radio, saying, "X-ray Hotel, this is Spooky 51 in orbit above you; looks like you could use a little help down there. I see lots of fireworks, over."

I responded, "Spooky 51, roger that. We're receiving rocket and automatic weapons' fire from both banks, but most of it from the north, over."

"Roger," he came back and said, "give me their coordinates. Let me know when you are clear and in what direction, over."

My response was, "Spooky 51, we are clear to the east, approximately a half-click. The fire came from YS122741 to YS119740, over."

"Standby," he said.

All at once tracer fire started pouring from the sky, saturating the area we had just passed through. It looked like a water hose of fire being sprayed from an unseen source in the sky. Total destruction. Didn't see how anyone above ground could survive that. Next, Seawolf gunships put in a close-up strike with rockets and mini-guns. They cleared the zone, providing air protection for us while artillery from an army firebase nearby put in another strike on both sides of the river.

Meanwhile, as our retaliation attack was going on, we had one man with a bullet through his leg and we were taking on water through our new rocket hole in the bow. While Shannon's boats were providing cover for us, our cover boat came alongside and tied up to keep us from sinking. As the crew shifted the weight from the front of the boat to the back in order to raise the bow, I put a pressure bandage on our crewmember's leg. Our boat captain took a poncho, rolled it up, crawled down in the bow and partially plugged the hole through which we were taking on water. That night we limped back to the base to deliver our wounded, and remove the boat from the water for repairs.

Chapter 14
LRRP Night Operations

The assignment tonight would be with the American army's Long Range Reconnaissance Patrol, called the LRRPs, the briefing officer told us. The LRRP's had a reputation for getting the job done. Most units had a South Vietnamese interpreter with them, a real big help with communications. Tonight we would take a squad of ten men to a location just outside a village on a small stream off the Soi Rap near Can Duoc. Intelligence reported that VC were out there waiting. The army's objective was to capture prisoners so that we could extract information about enemy activity in the area.

About 20:00 we were underway. It's a good thing our radar was in good working order; otherwise we wouldn't have been able to deliver the squad where it needed to go. The night was pitch black out, no stars showing. The stream was fifty or sixty feet wide with scant cover-- only patches on each side. We dropped the men off about 21:15, proceeded upstream a few hundred yards, turned around, and eased in alongside the bank. With our cover boat close in behind us, we tied up to some nipa palm alongside the stream to hold us in place. Then, we waited. Vietnamese voices were audible about 400 to 500 feet away, but we remained sitting there in silence, listening to every sound. About two hours later a flare popped over the location where we had dropped the LRRPs off, and we heard a lot of automatic weapon fire plus grenade explosions.

Our boat was less than a quarter mile from them. Within a few minutes they called us for extraction. We stripped the mooring lines from the nipa palm and headed for them. The flares kept the area illuminated, and both boats were on full alert, expecting any moment to be hit. When we arrived, we saw five or six bodies in the water and the LRRPs with two bags of documents they had taken. None of the Viet Cong was alive. No prisoners.

Then I saw it; a sampan about twelve-feet long beached alongside the bank containing a young girl. She was only about sixteen years old--and dead. Lying back over the tiller of the sampan, her face turned toward the sky, her eyes and arms open wide as though in some gesture of acceptance. The girl had no clothes on except for black pajama bottoms and a dirty brassiere. No blood was showing, as she lay there alone. This cannot be right, I said to myself. How is it even possible for someone this age to be involved in war? I didn't look her way again.

Then we loaded our boats with passengers. Mission completed. As we were backing out of the small stream, the light from the last flares was fading into darkness. Suddenly one of the officers riding with us opened up fire on the corpse of the young Vietnamese girl with our mounted M-60 machine gun. "What the hell did you do that for?" "She was dead anyway." I guess any justification will do in wartime.

Back at the base at 02:00, we called it a night. But I can't seem to get a certain dead child out of my mind.

Chapter 15
Friendly Fire from a South Vietnamese Outpost

There was a lot of distrust between some of the South Vietnamese and the Americans, especially in parts of the River Patrol Force. In most cases the local support personnel were difficult to work with.

Our tactical operations center had two or three Vietnamese radio operators who monitored communications when needed. Since their English was pretty good, they also acted as interpreters.

At daylight, our boats, returning from night patrol to our base at Nha Be, encountered small arms fire. Bullets hit the water near our boats and sang overhead from a South Vietnamese outpost across the river from our base. I picked up the radio handset and called, "Moon River, this is X-ray Hotel. We are receiving small arms fire from the friendly outpost across from your location. Contact them please and have them shut it off, over."

"Roger, X-ray Hotel," their answer came back.

But fire around our boats continued. Concerned, I picked up my radio handset once more. "Moon River, this is X-ray Hotel again. Tell those people to stop shooting at us or we are going to open fire and wipe out the whole damned compound, over."

"Roger," they came back. Shortly thereafter the firing stopped. Friendly fire we didn't need--we had enough to deal with, anyway.

Chapter 16
Night Ambush on the Long Tao

Our patrol left the base just before dark. Normally, we preferred to set up in our night location after it got dark enough to prevent our being seen entering it. Tonight we backed into a small stream about 20 feet wide that dumped into the Long Tao. The area, because it had been hit pretty hard by Agent Orange, was mostly bare of growing trees and brush. So we sat there quietly, radio turned down low and radar dimmed, watching the river for any activity. About two hours later, around 10:30 or so, a general broadcast came on the radio from an orbiting gunship. "We have one moving contact on the river at YS025668." I shined our red-lens covered flashlight on our chart to see where it was. Holy Jesus, it was within a few feet of where we were sitting! Just as I stood up, turning around with starlight scope in hand, a hostile sampan exited the small stream behind us. He saw us at the same time we saw him. Before we could get a shot off, he quickly turned the sampan upside down, got out of it and escaped into the darkness. Tonight he got away, but next time... He could have been VC or a local fisherman; it is uncertain. We fired a few rounds in his direction just to let him know it wasn't safe on the river at night during curfew. Sometimes these village fishermen stay out after dark, or prefer night fishing, and just get caught up in the war. Then they pay with their lives, which makes me sad.

Chapter 17
Duck Hunting on the Soi Rap

As our day patrol began, we loaded the boats with all the necessary supply replacements, ammo, C-rations, fuel and fresh water. Since more than one patrol used the same boat, these were routine duties prior to every departure. Today our briefing revealed only a few minor skirmishes overnight in our patrol areas.

The day was clear and the temperature comfortable. Our assignment was to check river traffic in the area southwest of Nha Be on the Soi Rap. We searched any and all sampans and boats for weapons and contraband that could be used to supply the Viet Cong. The traffic was light on the river and not much was happening.

A large flock of ducks flew over the boats as we sat drifting in the current. They landed about a thousand meters downstream from us in a wide section of the river. Probably sixty or seventy birds were present. After they got comfortable in the water, I picked up a M79 grenade launcher, adjusted the sight for about 300 meters, and told the coxswain and boat captain, "Let's go duck hunting." We cranked the boats; I got up on the bow, and braced myself. The boats headed full-speed ahead at our feathered enemy. When we got to within about 350 meters of the targets, I fired a single shot. When the shot sounded, the ducks immediately went airborne. My shot landed where they were sitting, and as the round hit the water, it exploded. Seven or eight ducks came tumbling back into the water.

My boat captain said, "Good shot, chief! Now what are you going to do with all them ducks?"

An old man in a sampan near the east bank was watching us closely. When he saw the duck hunt, he rowed out toward us. We met him with birds in hand. After being presented with all the ducks, he put both hands together, bowed and said *chow ohm*, which was thank you sir in his language. A good way to start the day.

That day we must have checked about thirty boats for contraband and ID papers. When I discovered an old radio that wouldn't work anymore, I gave it back to the owners. Overall it was a routine day, the river was pretty and calm, and it did not seem like a war zone. At least no one took a shot at us.

Chapter 18
Emergency LRRP Extraction

A few nights later we had a standard briefing prior to going on the river. Be alert, the army is experiencing heavy contact about six or seven clicks north of our patrol zones. So expect anything, we were told. After an hour on the river and darkness had set in, they called us back in for a quick briefing. The LRRPs of the army were in a bad spot about two miles north of our patrol zone and needed our help in getting out.

Two other patrols were called in to join ours, thus making six boats in all. Having received fire from several directions, the LRRPs had sporadic contact with several VC and were unsure which was the best way out. Moon River said via radio that they were at a bend in a small stream. Then they gave us the approximate coordinates. The stream was off the main Dong Tranh River and had several bends and turns in it.

We entered single file. The banks on each side of the narrow stream looked like a dense jungle. Our navigation charts did not show water depth; we weren't sure where the bottom was. The sky was clear and the moon was bright, as we slowly made our way back to the squad of men in distress. Within a few minutes, the Seawolves were airborne and providing overhead cover for us. Our patrol leader asked the LRRP patrol to pop a flare to mark its location.

They whispered back into the radio, "The VC are all over the place, flare going up." Since the LRRP popped a pistol flare over its position, that gave all of us a mark...including the VC. The creek was maybe thirty feet wide and narrowing, the farther back we went. My boats were the last two in the formation of six, and we were spaced about thirty to forty feet apart, hoping not to go aground while in a fight. We made sure everyone had flak jackets and helmets on with weapon in hand-- except the boat captains at the wheel. All of us in all six boats had every sense in our bodies "turned on." We were ready for the first muzzle flash of a weapon firing at us from either side of the stream. Then one of the LRRPs whispered into the radio in a hushed, confidential tone, "We can see you."

"Roger," the lead boat patrol officer came back, give me a blink on your flashlight to mark your location.

"O.K.," came back the reply.

All at once the Seawolves illuminated the area almost bright as day. It had a startling effect on all of us. I said, "Uh-oh, keep a close eye on those banks, guys," as we continued on upstream, slowing to a stop. There they were on the south side of the stream! The first four boats beached one at a time and took on the team, while all the others provided cover for them. The sky was still bathed in light from our air cover.

Now our problem was to turn around so we could get back out. The boats were thirty-one feet long, and the stream seemed about thirty feet wide. Using the boat hooks, we jockeyed with the engines and pulled on the brush to get turned around. Fortunately the water was deep enough. After everyone got turned, my boats led the way back out. As we proceeded cautiously back out towards the river, the flares faded to dark again. But we were not yet "out of the woods". After a few minutes the stream widened again, and I caught a glimpse of a silhouette in the moonlight, as the boat passed its earlier entrance. "Mac, is that you?" I asked on the radio, forgetting proper usage of radio procedure for a minute.

"Yeah, Jim, it's me. Just standing by in case you guys needed a little help," the voice came back. "Thanks," was my reply. We entered the main river, returned our passengers to the base and took a breather. Not a shot was fired, but we could feel hostile eyes on us-- the hair on the backs of our necks confirmed shoreline surveillance. Charlie knew that if anyone had fired on us, it would have been instant suicide for him. The enemy understood the rules of brown river fighting and let us pass.

Chapter 19
Village People Try to Make a Living

We were on day patrol a few days later near where the Dong Tranh branched off from the Long Tao. An old man had an unidentified object alongside his sampan. He motioned for us to come over to him. We did so, and as our boats came alongside we could see that he had a dead crocodile about twelve feet long bound lightly to his small boat. Through his broken English and our limited Vietnamese, we finally understood what he wanted. He begged us to tow that huge reptile to Saigon as a favor for him. Sorry, we can't haul crocodiles today. But we did use our machete and k-bar knives to help him cut up part of the large beast. When he left us with many thanks, his sampan was filled with enough crocodile meat to last a good while. What remained of the dead croc rested in the shallow water near the bank.

Our patrol now completed, we returned to the base later that evening. As several of us gathered in the chief's lounge over a cold beer, we went over the events of the day. Bob Faught spoke up and said he had thrown a concussion grenade on a large crocodile in that area but didn't know whether he had killed it or not.

Chapter 20
Cobra Snake Encounter
and a
Dud Grenade

On the Long Tao, we were drifting in the northern sector of our zone. There was little traffic on the river. The whole crew was enjoying the peace, but peace in a war zone is an illusion that can quickly disappear. Everyone was therefore keeping an eye out for trouble. It wasn't the two-legged enemy that caught us off-guard at the hanging tree that morning, however. It was man's oldest enemy, the snake.

Close to noon one of the boat crew spoke up, pointing, "Look at that!" Upstream from us, maybe a hundred feet or so, was a huge snake swimming across the river. It looked to be about ten feet long. One of the guys asked if he could take a few shots at it.

"Sure," I said, "go ahead." He put a M16 on semi-automatic and let off a few rounds. Since the bullets were hitting very close to him, he turned and started toward our boat. About twenty-five feet away and coming straight at us, the snake raised itself out of the water and flared its neck about eighteen inches above the surface. Now we know what it was: a cobra intent on getting into our boat. Boy, he looked mad and meant business! The hair raised on the back of my neck as I reached into our weapons locker, pulled out another M16, put it on full automatic and cut him in two pieces, just as he got to within six feet of the boat. Very spooky, to be attacked by a cobra from the water. Didn't we have enough enemies over here?

After that encounter a few fishermen in sampans came upon us. We checked them and let them pass. About an hour or so later just upstream from us we saw an old man and old woman in their sampan on one of the small streams on the south side of the river. Catching the tide high, they stretched nets across the little feeder streams. As the tide went out, they trapped a few fish in their nets. It looked like meager survival, at best.

We observed them working the stream. Soon, they were out of sight for about half an hour. Then we heard an explosion. Both boats moved close to the mouth of the feeder stream, but we couldn't make out anything. Standing orders forbade us to leave our boats, so we remained near the entrance. After thirty minutes or so, we saw the old man coming toward us in his sampan. Pulling up close, we saw his wife was dead and he was bleeding steadily from shrapnel wounds. From what we could get from him, as we towed his sampan and dead wife back to our base for medical assistance, she had picked up a live M79 grenade that had been fired but did not did not explode on impact. Can you believe it? She had been killed by a dud grenade. An innocent would-be fisherman lost his wife and was seriously hurt himself. In a war zone, it seems like the innocent are more in danger than the guilty.

Chapter 21
VC Ambush

Our crews prepared for night patrol on the Soi Rap, loading up all the necessary things into our boats. The patrol officers and boat captains went to briefing to let us in on all the latest intelligence. Before we were dismissed, we were told that tonight we had a new Ltjg. Tactical Officer in our tactical operations center [TOC]. I didn't give it much thought, as we finished briefing and went on to our assigned area of patrol.

Arriving on location, our position was coded and called in to TOC so they would know our whereabouts. The cover boat came alongside and tied up. Both boats drifted together, as we sometimes did during daylight hours, the sun still in the sky. Usually the contact was just for the company and conversation between the crews.

As the sun was going down, we looked out to the west and saw the silhouettes of two water buffalo grazing near the river, unconcerned that a war was going on around them. More innocents in the midst of fighting. Everything was quiet. The sun disappeared, and soon darkness was upon us. Our boats moved apart for defense--together we were a large, inviting target. Because there was no place we could tie up alongside the banks to observe the river, we dropped anchor about fifty feet from the west bank.

Around 21:00 after darkness had been on us an hour or so, a coded message came through that X-ray Juliet, Bob Faught's patrol, would be transiting the narrow waterways from his patrol area on the Long Tao River to my location on the Soi Rap. Bob called my patrol and ask if I had copied and understood Moon River's message to him.

I answered in the affirmative. Then he came on the radio again and said, "Jim, standby, we may need your help."

"We are ready," was my reply.

He was about to do the impossible. At night in unfamiliar territory with streams branching off in several directions, Bob was proceeding through a high-risk area with only two PBRs and no helicopter gunship coverage. If your radar went out in there, you could easily go aground and present an exposed, stationary target. Not a good feeling. Seven miles separated us from Bob's patrol.

Quickly pulling anchor, we moved out to midstream. I checked our chart to plot a course if we had to go into the swamp after him.

About twenty minutes later, where his patrol would be, there was tracer fire. Heavy, heavy contact about three miles away. He came on the radio, called Moon River, our TOC for help, saying his patrol was under attack from heavy automatic weapons' fire. He requested Seawolf support and the help of X-ray Hotel. Acknowledging his call for help, we floor-boarded it to his patrol. I hurriedly asked Bob his chart coordinates and said we were on our way "at best speed."

He replied, "I don't know Jim, I think we're lost." As our boats entered another offshoot of the river heading to where we thought he might be, his firing had ceased and he called us back and said, "X-ray Hotel, we have wounded. We've turned around and are going back out the way we came in, we hope. So you can abort the assistance run, and thanks! Will see you back at camp, over."

"Roger, Juliet," was my reply. We slowed down just before we got to a hairpin turn in the stream and turned both boats around, allowing our cover boat to lead us back out to the Soirap. As we completed our turn around, we began receiving automatic weapons' fire. It came from six or seven positions on the south bank of the hairpin turn that we were fast approaching. We gave them back about forty or fifty rounds from our .50 cal. deck gun mounted on the stern of our boat, as we exited the kill zone. That was a little too close.

Bob's patrol had gone right into an ambush and had suffered casualties; within a few seconds, we would have been in an ambush and probably also taken several casual-

71

ties. That was a very foolish decision coming from TOC that night. The Seawolves had been out on another call at the time and therefore had been unable to respond to X-ray Juliet's call for help.

After returning to the base, I looked up Bob Faught and asked him about the fight. He said the VC were really bold. Several of them were just standing erect on the bank, firing at almost point-blank range until he opened up with his .50s. As his boats returned fire, he witnessed their bodies being torn up and blown to bits. One of his men, the forward .50 gunner, had an AK47 round pass through the gun tub, ending up in his stomach about three inches below his navel. Fortunately the round was almost spent and only penetrated about a quarter inch.

After his boats were clear, his gunner reached down and squeezed the bullet out and said, "Man, that was close! A couple of inches lower and my family jewels would have really been in trouble." A few more of his crew were wounded slightly. Two rounds hit the back of our boat, but thankfully no one was hurt.

Chapter 22
F-100 Shock Bomb Awakening.
We are the Bait

Various areas of the rivers had to be patrolled differently because of the width, the natural defenses, such as tree cover, the depth of the water, or because of known VC staging areas. Sometimes we would anchor in the middle of the river when the banks were clear, and there was nothing to tie up to or to conceal us. Tonight we anchored our boats in the middle of the Long Tao.

Nights got very long. If everything was still quiet after we had sat a few hours, we would take turns keeping watch while others in the crew caught a little sleep or relaxed from the ever-present fatigue.

We rested at anchor in the river near the entrance of the stream leading back into the swamp where Bob Faught's patrol had had its recent contact. At 02:00 we were all very tired. I had relaxed on the engine covers and had fallen asleep. All at once, we were startled awake by the US Air force. We were not sure if they were USN or USAF, but two F100s were surely in the sky. Five shock bombs went off about a thousand meters from where we were anchored. 20mm cannons were also to be heard.

First, I thought we ourselves were under attack by our own pilots. The planes made three more passes at their target, dropping napalm and shock bombs. The concussion and the fire were awesome to behold. Just tremendous. I called Moon River, our TOC, about the strike and asked if there was something we should know about it. They replied SLAR and Red Haze [types of ground detection equipment in an orbiting aircraft] had confirmed that thirty or forty VC were detected advancing toward our boats.

"That was another close one, Chief! Looks like Charlie's

spies spotted us and were setting us up, and we were the bait," stated my boat captain.

As I gazed at the dark sky my reply was, "Someone must be looking out for us." We pulled anchor and remained in the area a while longer, watching and listening for movement that didn't come. Our patrol was scheduled to end around 04:30. We headed back to the base forty-five minutes early, so the next patrol could use the boats.

Chapter 23
Sniper in a Tree

As we were preparing for our night patrol, our briefing officer informed us that intelligence had reported something strange. An all-female sapper team of Viet Cong was operating in our area. That caught our attention, because we did not like to fire our weapons at women. Chivalry, I guess. Although female VC were considered to be some of the enemy's fiercest fighters. This all made cold chills go up my back. Anyway, we were duly warned.

Arriving at our assigned area on the Soi Rap about two hours before dark, we checked out where we would be setting up for the night. A few sampans floated by, mostly trying to get back home before night came. Our boats were drifting out about a hundred yards from the bank on the west side of the river with the engines shut off-- as we frequently did. All was deathly quiet. I was standing and had my back turned to the wooded shoreline. All at once, it was if a strong, unseen hand had forced me to sit down on the engine covers behind me. As I did so, a bullet zipped over my head, hitting the water thirty or forty feet out in front of me. (The bullet passed by where my head had been just a few moments previously.) From the trees back off the river, I had heard the familiar "pop" sound. Someone had seen us, but we couldn't see them. Since we were unsure where the shot came from, we moved out of the area downstream.

It was getting close to sunset. After all the light of the day had faded into the west, we moved back upstream where the sniper had taken a shot at us. Again we drifted in the current, as my boat captain and I scanned the bank and trees beyond the bank with binoculars and starlight scope. [Note: The starlight scope gathers existing light and magnifies it many times to give a clear and magnified image]. I had the starlight scope trained on a large tree about 200 feet back from the water's edge just as someone in the tree lit a cigarette. The scope is so sensitive to light, the fire from the burning tobacco looked like a torch in the tree. I told our crews, "The sniper's in the large tree about 200 feet back."

Handing one of the crew the starlight scope, I said, "Don't fire! Let's try something first, since he probably can't see us clearly, even though he may be able to make out the boats." Our man trained the scope on the tree and confirmed he could see the glow from the cigarette. I picked up a M79 grenade launcher, changed the sights on it, and set in 200 meters as the range to the targeted tree. Quickly I aimed at the tree and fired. The grenade went off in the tree about where the cigarette had been seen lit a few minutes earlier. No more sniper rounds received from that area, and we had only fired a single round in return.

Just after midnight we completed our patrol on the Soirap. There was no further contact with the enemy. On our way back to the base at a fast rate of speed, we went into a right curve in the river. There one of our crewmembers tapped me on the shoulder, pointing to something over on the port side, maybe 500 feet back from the river's edge. He asked, "What do you think that is, Chief?" I took the binoculars, did a double take and said, "Wait a minute, guys! Are we seeing what I think we have in our sights?" Without a word, we all realized it was a round, silvery object about 150 feet in diameter, suspended about 100 feet from the ground. I picked up the radio handset and said, "Hotel One, [our cover boat] we are making a left turn to check out something on the north bank, over."

"Roger, you see it too," was his reply.

As we turned to get a closer look, it stayed in place, hovering as we talked among ourselves. Was it a flying saucer? Not sure, I was certainly not going to take a shot at it. We agreed among ourselves only to report it back at TOC, and not over the radio. After observing it intently for a few minutes, we turned and continued on to the base. As the crews took care of the boats, I went to TOC, expecting ridicule. When I reported the sighting to the duty officer, he said others had seen the same object tonight. He did not know what it was either, but hesitated sending the Seawolves to check it out. I'm not sure if he ever did. And after leaving the center I heard nothing further of our mystery sighting.

Chapter 24
Charlie Sends in a few Mortar Rounds

After spending seventy-odd hours a week on the rivers, a day off from time to time helped to refresh us. It allowed us to catch up on our correspondence, especially writing home. In all my letters home I did not mention the firefights or near misses we had had. Instead, I tried to concentrate on the less dangerous and destructive aspects of my tour with the River Patrol Force. It was my desire that my wife worry no more than absolutely necessary. Sometimes, for sure, she could see through my attempts at playing down the eventful nights and days on the river.

After writing home and getting caught up on all that was happening around the base compound and chief's quarters, my wanderings led me to the mess hall about noon. I sat down with Chief McGowan, one of my friends and a distinguished patrol officer. He inquired, "Jim, have you seen that old man outside the base in the village who can tell fortunes and read your past and future?"

"No, I haven't," was my reply.

He said, "That old man is amazing. He looks to be about eighty years old. He told me things I did when I was a kid. And he even knew things about my family. You have just got to go see him."

"I don't know Mac, I don't believe in this kind of thing. But I am curious, after what you say he told you about your life. Where can he be found?" I asked.

I walked outside the gate and down the main street to look for him. Since the village of Nha Be was not very big, I thought he should be easy to find. The streets were crowded with guys from the base compound from all the US services. Lots of street vendors were trying to sell the GI something.

After looking around for a while, I spotted an old man sitting at a small table on the sidewalk with an empty chair before him. As I came nearer, he spoke in broken English, "You are looking for me, please sit." This was a bit startling to me; still I sat down as invited.

He said, "I will give you a reading of your past life for $3.00, or a full life for $5.00. But before you decide, know that there are many people who have sought me out to read for them. I have traveled the world." In his gnarled hands he held a large book, well worn and seemingly ancient. It was over two inches thick, about the size of a large encyclopedia.

"In here are names of leaders and rulers from all over the world. The King of Saudi Arabia is one, General Eisenhower is another. Some have authority and power, others do not. But you may look, if you like," he said.

I thumbed through it. With its many languages and signatures, it certainly looked authentic enough. I was still suspicious, however. Was this just a hoax to get my money?

"Give me your $3.00 reading, if you will please," I said, as he closed the book in front of him.

Touching both of my hands, he proclaimed, "This is you, at the age of four. You almost died. You come from a poor but honorable heritage. You are married and have two children. Your wife loves you very much and is very concerned for you. You must stop drinking or it can consume you. You will live to be 68-70 years old, but you must be very careful. Much danger is in your path, but you will survive. You will complete your service and in your later years you will open a business, but it will fail. You will be happy and content. Do not forget care and concern for others." These things he wrote on a piece of paper, even as he told them to me.

I paid him the three dollars and thanked him. As I walked away, I remembered: when I was four years old, I cut my right knee with a butcher knife while trying to make a rubber gun. My mom told me I had nearly bled to death. Yes, I am married and have two children. As for the drinking, I had not had any that day, but there was indeed a bottle of whiskey in my locker. From it I would take a big swig after a harrowing firefight. Once in a while, I'd have three or four beers before going to bed, when I knew I had the next day off. The old soothsayer was on target so far; as for future danger, we would have to wait and see.

The same night around 20:30 three mortar rounds hit Nha Be, and two hit our compound. The gates were closed, no one was allowed in and no one out, while full alert and defense of the base were in effect. Seawolves were scrambled and went airborne. All available boats were to get underway, and all boats out on patrol were called in for perimeter protection. Until we knew what was going on, we reinforced our perimeter guards all around the base. The alert lasted about two hours. Nothing was found; the VC had apparently lobbed in a few mortar shells from across the river before he had fled.

While we were still on full alert and instructed to remain in chief's quarters, one chief came into the lounge where most of us were gathered. He was wet, covered with sewage and smelling like a sewer. We asked him what had happened. He said, "When those rounds hit, I was out in the village and those damned VC out guarding the gate wouldn't let me back in. So I went to the water's edge and was going to wade through the muck and mud to get back here. It was up to my neck, and I had to swim part of the way. I wasn't going to die out there like that. Damn near got shot by a marine, as I came ashore down near the other side of the helicopter pad. I need to take a shower, guys, if you'll excuse me."

Chapter 25
Move to Ben Luc

Admiral Zumwalt, Commander of Naval Forces in Vietnam, our river squadron commander, and the powers that be decided that River Division 591 would be moved from Nha Be to Ben Luc up on the Vam Co Dong River. Now we were to join Operation Giant Slingshot. We would be patrolling and setting up a blocking force between the Parrot's Beak of Cambodia and Saigon. Our base of operations was to be the *USS Harnett County* [LST-821], an old LST that was primarily to be used for living quarters and support for the river divisions operating in the area. After a few days we had made our complete move and were out running patrols.

The river was much narrower than the ones we had previously patrolled. The Vam Co Dong had not been defoliated. Dense stands of nipa palm, trees and other brush grew along the riverbanks with very few breaks. We will be easy targets, and in some places pointblank range, I thought as we proceeded up river.

My first patrol was with Bob Faught, my friend and a fine patrol officer who had distinguished himself many times. During the move Bob and his patrol had preceded ours by a few weeks. By now he was fairly familiar with the terrain and the differences in the type of patrols we would have to run.

About two hours before dark he told both of my boat crews much that they had not experienced before. He warned us about the tides in this narrow river. He told us, "The water level has a range of ten to twelve feet rise and fall. When the tides come in, the water runs upstream. When it goes out, the current is pretty swift. The boats can go aground quickly if you are tied up alongside the bank in a shallow area. Also, be prepared to get shot at more often

81

than we did at Nha Be! It's a whole new war zone, and they are out to kill us. Remember the $2000.00 reward on our heads at Nha Be? I don't know if it applies here or not. They just want us dead. Be cautious! Know where you are at all times! We think sometimes they walk the banks of the river just looking for a PBR to toss a grenade into."

We tied up to a heavy nipa palm to our starboard side; the river was to our port side as we faced upstream. Keeping an eye on the river with the starlight scope, we saw that all was quiet. After a long day we were dead tired.

Bob said, "Jim, get a little rest, I will keep an eye out."

I thanked him and lay down on the engine covers.

About half an hour or so later, Bob put his hand on my shoulder, gave me a quick shake, and said quietly, "Listen!" He pointed to the nipa palm. We could hear the sounds of walking and whispers in Vietnamese about fifteen feet away. I picked up a M16, Bob had one, and one of the crew on the M-60. When we thought the time was right, I opened up with the M16, realizing it probably wouldn't penetrate the nipa palm. The others started firing, also. Bob tossed a grenade up and over the nipa palm, as we broke ambush and headed upstream.

A secondary explosion was audible, as the grenade Bob threw went off. It appeared Charlie had pulled the pin on one for us and was unable to get it off. Meanwhile, as I pulled the trigger on the first burst of gunfire, I lost my balance and ended up on my butt.

Bob said, "Good show, Jim! I thought you got shot." Our patrol reset itself a few hundred yards upstream and the remainder of the patrol was relatively quiet. About the time our patrol was due to end, another sound came from the nipa palm we were tied up to. I picked up my M16 again and fired toward the sound. I yelled back to our cover boat behind us, "Let's get out of here!" Both boat engines coming alive, we headed up river.

Bob told me, "Congratulations, Jim, you just fell for the same thing I did. You just shot at a monkey. Near daylight, you can hear them near the banks foraging for food. Sometimes they can fool you." Our shift was almost over for the night, so we headed on back to our temporary home anchored in the river.

Just off the starboard side of our home, the *Harnett County*, the Seabees were sending water and sand from the bottom of the river into a swampy area near the village of Ben Luc. They were literally pumping a base for us up out of the river. Water and sand pushed in, the sand stayed and the water ran back into the river, leaving a solid landfill. It worked and it worked well. We could see it growing daily, as we went about our duties.

The river division personnel lived on board the *Harnett County* in tight living quarters, and our boats were tied up at the boat booms extending from each side of the ship. Climbing up and down the booms on rope ladders, lowering things needed for patrol by rope, and running fuel hoses down the boom for refueling were part of our daily routine while the pier was being built upstream from the ship.

The river where the ship anchored was not much wider than the length of the ship. Downstream from the anchorage were thick nipa palm, other trees and brush on both sides of the river. Out beyond the river were the fields and rice paddies with patches of undergrowth. The cover allowed Charlie to take shots at the ship from both sides of the river. Sniper shots were almost routine. On one occasion he fired a rocket that penetrated the ship, went through the wardroom, did some damage and exploded in the captain's cabin. Several crewmembers were hit with shrapnel, but no-one was killed. All PBRs sitting alongside were scrambled to get them underway for ship defense. And those on nearby patrol were called in closer until we determined what Charlie was up to. The Viet Cong and the enemy in Saigon wanted the Harnett County sunk and the river patrol boats she was supporting destroyed, because we were hurting them too much. We were restricting their flow of men and materials in the war effort, and this was the very purpose of Giant Slingshot. The operation was intended to prevent infiltration by enemy forces.

Several times each month all the units were scrambled for perimeter defense. Often the ship would shift anchorage a few hundred yards, mostly at night, because we feared Charlie would sight in a rocket during the day, then come back at night and fire it. At high tide the ship was visible for quite a distance, so it could not remain stationary for any length of time.

Mines were a major concern. Charlie might float them down river to sink our boats when were not on patrol. Deck watches were set with loaded weapons; we were on alert for anything at all suspicious floating toward the ship. Often we tossed a concussion grenade into the water just to discourage any swimmers.

A survey of the area by Admiral Zumwalt and our superior officers from the air revealed that a lot of the trees and brush had to be removed because Charlie could hide behind them in a sniper position. So Operation Chop-Chop was formed, in order to remove all enemy cover. Those not on patrol formed working parties. Each day two men from my boat crews were used, alternating with others in our boats. Approximately sixty men per day chopped down nipa palm, trees, brush and everything standing, as far back as 2,000 feet downstream from the ship.

It took at least a month of chop-chop parties and guards protecting them to clear most of the foliage. My crews assisting with the cutting said it was tough working that hard. One of them said, "Chief, this is almost like being on the chain gang in Georgia, clearing the right of way for roads." Their blisters and dark suntans confirmed it.

Our boats alternated with other patrols on the river, protecting the area of the chop-chop party, so that Charlie wouldn't set up booby traps at night while they were off work.

Meanwhile several of the patrols, including my own, had sporadic contact with the VC on other parts of the river. The days and nights were long, often very wet and filled with uncertainty as to where the next attack might originate. Other US Navy river boats, including RAG boats, Monitors,

Zippos, Douche Boats, Tango Boats, and others were often seen transiting our patrol areas, doing their part in this war.

Map 2

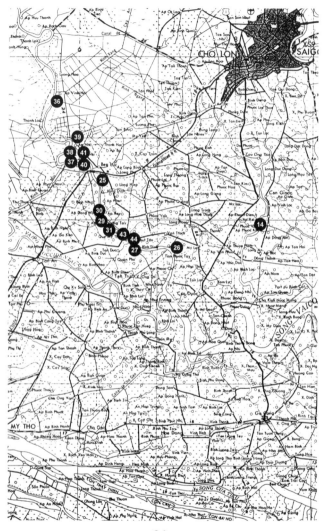

Chapter 26
SEALS and Friendly Fire from the US Army

At our briefing prior to the night patrol, our briefing officer said we would be working with the SEAL team. Tonight we support them in one of their night operations. The team consisted of seven men. We waited until about 21:30 to leave the pier, transporting them down river some seven miles to a location the team leader had selected. The VC were using five or six hutches about 500 meters back off the river, intelligence said. The Seals were to check them out and gather more intelligence, if possible. In the bend of the river they had selected, the banks were covered with thick nipa palm and brush. We found a small opening and nosed the boats into the bank.

The team leader asked that we protect their backs from the dangers of the river; they would call us when ready to extract. Disembarking over the bow of the boats, the SEALS disappeared soundlessly into the night. We quietly backed out and moved both boats upstream about a hundred yards and tied up to the nipa palm extending out over the water.

All was quiet for a few hours. Suddenly, we heard several bursts of M16 gunfire in the area where the SEALS were active. Then quiet, no radio-call at all. So we simply waited and listened. Hours passed, and daylight was approaching. As light broke in the east, one of my crewmen had to use the restroom. Since our boats are only thirty-one feet long, we don't have the luxury of a restroom. Therefore we take our relief over the back of the boat. He had his pants down, hanging it over the stern of the boat, with his naked butt exposed. About that time artillery shells started falling in the river about 150 yards from us and moved on across to where the SEALS had gone in. Shrapnel and chunks of mud were flying through the air, some of it hitting our boats. "Get down," I yelled to everyone. Our exposed crewman pulled his pants back up and climbed back over the stern for cover.

We were not sure what was happening or who was responsible for it. Both boat captains were directed to get underway at top speed and to move southerly of where we had been in the main stream. I quickly picked up the radio handset, called our tactical operations center and announced that we were under an artillery attack and that rounds are falling very close to us. A voice told me they originated at a US Army firebase in Tan An province. Since we didn't have their radio frequency, I asked for help in contacting that base. I yelled, "Tell them to shut it off, please! We have personnel ashore here, and mud and shrapnel are hitting our units." It took about a minute, but it stopped, much to our relief. About thirty rounds in all had fallen. To our good fortune, none of them were air bursts.

Light was increasing in the east. The SEAL team called for extraction, so we moved back into the same opening, nosed in and picked them up. The team leader asked, "What was happening with that artillery? It was falling close to us, too. We were worried about you guys out here escaping it."

I explained what had happened and asked him how it had gone for them. He said, "We had to kill five. But we did get the documents we were after. A young boy almost blew it for us, though. When he came out of a hutch to take a leak, he saw us. We had to immobilize him, tie him up and tape his mouth shut so he wouldn't give us away. We let him go when we left."

We backed out and started upstream at full speed, heading northwest. About ten minutes into the trip, I chanced to look back at our cover boat racing along the water. All at once a single rocket came at it, fired from the north bank. Luckily it missed the boat by a few feet and fell into the water without exploding. We did not return fire because our boats were already moving out of range.

Chapter 27
SEALS and Booby Traps

The following night we were assigned to work with the SEALS again, this time at a different location. SEAL intelligence had located a cache of weapons and explosives. Their mission was simple: investigate and destroy. Around 21:30 we loaded up and took them to the exact coordinates they wanted. This time there were eight members of the SEAL team. We nosed both boats quietly into the bank on the south side of the river where the nipa palm and undergrowth were lightest. Our passengers slid off the bow of the boats and silently disappeared into the darkness. We backed out and went upstream a short distance so that we wouldn't betray their location. After only a few minutes the team leader double- clicked the radio and whispered into it, "Shapeless Two Zero, [My new call sign since we had moved up to Ben Luc], pick us up now!"

My response, "Roger, give me a light when you see me, over."

"Roger," he came back.

Quietly we slipped back down the 100 yards or so, and as he blinked his red light, both boats nosed back in. The SEALS came back aboard. When the last man was on board he said, "Let's get out of here." We backed out and floorboarded it, heading up river.

The SEAL team leader explained, "We were walking into a bunch of booby traps, trip wires-- and what else we're not sure. But we can fix that. Can I use your radio?"

"Sure," was my reply, while getting out of his way.

Picking up the radio handset, he said, "Shapeless, [our tactical operations center] this is Insertion One, I want a Redleg strike at my previous insertion coordinates. You've got the numbers. We're clear. Fire when ready, we will spot, over."

They acknowledged his call and about two minutes later we were 500 meters or so up river, watching. Having slowed both boats, we were maintaining station in the middle of the river. Suddenly the whole south side of the river for 100 yards on each side of where we had picked them up lit up with a heavy barrage of artillery. Right on target! The strike came from the Tan An firebase that had almost hit us the night before. Several large secondary explosions resounded during the strike. Time for us to depart and head on back up river.

Chapter 28
The Anti-Vietnamese Boatswain

My boat captains and crews changed fairly often. Sometimes they would be promoted, transferred to other patrols, or hurt in battle-- so I apologize to them for not remembering names. I do remember, however, that every man I served with was deserving of the term: Man of Valor. Not a single time did I have a crewmember who was afraid to take on the Viet Cong in enemy territory.

A new boat captain was assigned to me, and as usual, I wanted new men to ride with me the first few times on patrol so we could find out about each other. He was a Boatswain Mate Second Class from another river division. Firmly, he let it be known that he wasn't afraid of anyone on the river.

We worked together about three weeks and I got to see him "in action." Toward the local people he demonstrated an attitude of contempt. Diplomatically, I suggested that he treat them with a little more respect. After all, we shouldn't forget that it was still their country. We would pass sampans on the river at a high rate of speed. Normally we would give them a wide berth so the wake of our boats would not bother them. But he preferred to pass them close, sometimes leaving the occupants of these small boats struggling to stay afloat. After calling him down on it three or four times with little effect, my patience was wearing thin.

Soon we were proceeding upstream from Ben Luc to relieve another patrol on station. An old man alone in his sampan was coming downstream near the bank just north of the Ben Luc bridge. My new boat captain saw him, and while at full speed, steered the PBR over to within a few feet of the old fellow. Then he made a sharp left half-turn. Our wake swamped the man's sampan and pitched him into the river. I demanded of my comrade, "Why did you do that?"

His reply was, "South Vietnamese, North Vietnamese,

Viet Cong. They're all the same. There's absolutely no difference between them. Damn them all!"

I said, "Let me drive," and took the wheel. Slowing down, I looked back and saw with joy that the old man was alive and had righted his boat.

Our patrol concluded without much activity, except for a few fruitless searches. Back home, after tying up to the pier, my first stop was to the office of the River Division CO. "Mr. Declercq, how do you fire a boat captain?" I asked with feeling.

"Tell him he's fired. Bring him in here, and we will all three talk about it."

After writing out our patrol report, I went back down to the pier, where he was still working on the boat, and told him the skipper wanted to see both of us right now. After our talk, my boat captain requested immediate transfer to a RAG. He could thereby avoid being written up and having a negative record. All agreed, and it was arranged like he had wanted.

GMG2 Castro was my next boat captain. Promoted from boat gunner to boat captain, he had recently seen a lot of action with me. We worked well together. Also assigned to us was a guy fresh-out-of-PBR-school-and-in-country-ready-to-win-the-war-tonight. Had I ever been like that? I couldn't even remember.

Chapter 29
Aground at Night

Sometimes the monsoon rains were so intense the pumps in the boat's bilges never seemed to stop. Without the pumps, the engines would've flooded out. Today we were on patrol up river from our base of operations, and it had been raining most of the day. Approaching the bridge at Ben Luc, we saw a familiar sight. A wire net was in place part-way across the river to prevent mines from being floated down river. Such mines could damage the bridge and ships anchored nearby.

Today, in the hellish, heavy rains on return from patrol we saw that the net had caught something. It was not mines, however, but three Vietnamese bodies. All were tangled in the wire net. One was a naked man, about forty years old, bloated, floating on his back. His hands, arms and legs lay stretched open, as if he were making some futile reach for the sky. The other two, floating farther away in the rushing current, wore black clothing. The surging water held this pair of corpses against the net.

Death, which comes in so many forms in this country, never gets any easier to take. I won't forget this sight. The silent, understanding nods among our men meant only one thing: We wanted this war to stop so we could go home.

The day patrols were usually routine, involving searches and control of river traffic. Usually a few sampans were on the river near the town of Ben Luc. But not many boats traversed the river in the daytime south of the village. Ground troops making a sweep of an area near the river sometimes used us as a blocking force.

It was time to make preparations for the night. Our briefing informed us where each patrol would be on the river. Location of others was crucial because, if an emergency occurred, we could move quickly to their aid.

All communications dealing with tactics and patrol positions were transmitted in a frequently changing code. Charlie was always listening. Thus, any information he might possibly use had to be disguised. For example, we said, "Shapeless One Nine, this is Shapeless Two Zero, Shackle BZY XLB RSH LXC Unshackle." This meant that the codes were to be revealed by using the same code book that we were issued at predetermined dates and times. But if we were in a firefight and timing was critical, everything was transmitted not in code, but "in the clear." Our lives depended upon the speed of information transfer.

Our night patrol set up about three miles south of Ben Luc, where Mitch Wells' patrol had spotted a sampan before. It appeared to be loaded with army troops who had got away. Mitch sure didn't miss many. This time he did, however, because he was some distance away when the enemy emerged. He passed along the necessary information to us.

After running the length of our patrol zone and part way back, we eased into the bank near the previous sighting. Darkness was setting in. Both boats tied up to a nipa palm in order to hold our place in the current. To minimize our profile and to make us look like a part of the riverbanks at night, our crews cut large pieces of palm and draped them across the boats. This tactic must have worked, because our own passing patrols boats even missed us at times. Then we would reveal ourselves--since we didn't need friendly fire on the river! Tonight we sat there, waiting for a sampan crossing, but nothing happened. A couple of hours passed and one of the crew said quietly, "Chief, look over the side." The tide had taken the water out from under us, and we were about eight or ten feet from the main stream of the river. Most important, we were sitting in the mud.

"Not good, guys. We're sitting ducks," I said. I called back to our cover boat, about thirty feet behind us, with a coded message which, when broken down and decoded, stated, Aground, increase alert, remain silent, wait for tide.

He responded with, "Roger that."

The same message went to our TOC. There was no choice but to sit there, on full alert, until the tide came back in and re-floated us. I must admit we were a bit apprehensive, but our waiting paid off. The water ran upstream as the tide returned; soon thereafter we were again afloat. Not at all easy on the nerves, sitting for four hours in the mud! No, no fun at all to be without mobility. Fortunately no-one spotted us, and the target sampan didn't show up either. The patrol ended after we cleaned the mud out of the Jacuzzi pumps and were able, again, to get underway.

Chapter 30
Night Patrol with Army Team and Sampans

Soon thereafter we learned that an army squad from the 101ª Airborne would ride out with us on a night ambush. Four of their men and their lieutenant came aboard my boat and our cover boat took the other five guys. The area we chose was close to where we had earlier gone aground. This time, however, I checked the tide tables so we wouldn't be left high and dry again. We were snugly in alongside the bank with brush partly covering us. About two hours after setting up, one of our crew tapped me on the shoulder, pointing behind us. To our rear a sampan was entering a small stream. The two-man crew was really rowing hard. As they disappeared from view, I told the lieutenant and my men to be prepared, "Those two are testing to see if it's safe to cross the river."

My boat captain scanned the horizon with the starlight scope, soon saying, "Chief, here they come! Two sampans, three in the first, and four in the second."

"Wait until they are committed to the crossing before we illuminate them," I said. After they had moved out to about midstream, we cast off the brush, released our moorings and cranked the engines. Pulling away from the bank, we lit up the sampans with three flares. Before the light was bright enough to see them clearly, bursts of automatic weapons' fire came upon us. It was our intention to capture prisoners and to take whatever documents they were carrying. But these men had chosen instead to fight.

When the muzzles of three or four automatic weapons flashed toward us, I said in a loud voice, "Fire!" The army guys all started firing, joined by a couple of my men, who held M16s and M60s. The cover boat did the same. I yelled,

"Cease fire," when things seemed to get out of hand. My boat captain and I kept the enemy illuminated with flares. Suddenly the VC jumped out of the boats, dumping them so that neither documents nor weapons would be found. Next they plunged underwater, with the aim of swimming back to shore. As they attempted to evade us, we tossed two concussion and one frag grenade where they were last seen.

The situation was awkward for our boat crews. With almost no chance of capturing prisoners, everyone was firing at two boats. My instructions were to rake with fire the bank they had left in hopes of eliminating the snipers who sought out crossing boats. No additional fire was heard tonight, and the patrol ended about 01:30. Thankfully there were no casualties--only a couple of rounds had struck our boats. It was the VC who had lost everything.

Chapter 31
Night Ambush, Under God's Protection

Preparations for night patrol were routine. As we learned where the others patrols would be setting up on the river, intelligence had news that might affect us. As night fell, we pulled into the bank and made ourselves look like part of the surrounding area. About half an hour later a couple of RAG boats passed us on their way upstream. We acknowledged our location to them, as they went on their way. Everything was quiet, and we had been in ambush about two hours.

Call it instinct, foresight, or whatever, but I yelled out to our cover boat, which was only a few feet behind us, "Let's get out of here now! Head up stream fast as you can!" We dumped our camouflage brush, cranked the boats and slammed the throttles hard foreword-- as everyone followed my orders. Clearing the area we had been in about one minute ago, a salvo of artillery from one of the nearby US Army firebases dropped right where we had been sitting in ambush. This attack sure made all of us nervous. Just imagine: friendly fire coming this close to wiping out all eleven of us! Even more nerve shattering than an attack from Charlie.

Proceeding upstream near some old water barges anchored in the river, we had time to discuss what had just happened. My cover boat captain asked, "Chief, how did you know we were in danger?"

My response was, "I didn't know. I was getting uncomfortable with us sitting there, and before I knew it, the words spilled out that we should get the hell out of there. It certainly looks as though the Lord was looking out for us. Guys, we'll be protecting those water barges for the rest of our patrol, so get tied up and keep an eye out!" About three hours later our patrol ended and we went on back to the pier, tied up and called it a night. This time I took a big swig from the bottle in my locker before going to bed, still a bit nervous about the near miss from friendly fire. Mistakes like this seemed to be happening with ever-greater frequency.

Chapter 32
Medical Treatment for some of the Local Villagers

The crew welcomed a day patrol. At briefing, we learned about our new daytime assignment, as one chief and two hospital corpsmen looked on. Today we were to stop at three small settlements on the river to render medical assistance to all those who would accept it from us. For help in communication with the locals, we took along a Vietnamese interpreter.

Most of the people feared us, but some brought hurt or sick children out to us. I couldn't help but think of my own kids back in the States. Our corpsmen treated the Vietnamese children, giving them antibiotics for infections. One little girl about ten years old came forth with large sores on her left arm and left leg. It appeared that she had been cut. I demanded that the interpreter find out the origin of her wounds. "Who did this to you?" I had him ask. "The VC," she replied. That child was hurting, but the chief corpsman assured me she would be all right after treatment. She had been injured about three days earlier when a group of Viet Cong came into her village and ransacked it, roughing up some villagers and murdering others.

I resolved not to show them any mercy when we met again. And that meeting was only a matter of time. Today, we felt we had done some good, and that seemed to shorten the trip back to base.

Chapter 33
Anti-Aircraft 40mm
Artillery Strike

The *USS Harnett County* (LST 821) was still our home. I want to cite here what Commander Schreadly has to say about the good ship and crew we knew: "The threat to the *Harnett County* from enemy and sapper attack was constant, and the ship was struck by both rocket and recoilless rifle fire.... A number of the crew was wounded by shrapnel" (*From the Rivers to the Sea*, 191). I came to know the bravery, and genius, of their gun crews and fire control officer, and grew to admire them all greatly.

The ship had 40mm anti-aircraft guns mounted on both sides of the bridge, as well as on the bow and stern. Usually, while at sea, these guns offer protection from enemy aircraft. When firing at aircraft, they employ high explosive, self-destroying tracer ammunition for proximity kills.

It was just after sunset, and my patrol found itself in a bend in the river north of Ben Luc. No problems so far. Our location was about two miles northwest of the *Harnett County*. Mitch Wells, one of my friends and a fellow patrol officer, was receiving automatic weapons' fire from a known bunker area. He called the attack in, and as his patrol sailed upriver to the northwest, away from the bunkers, the message came back to him, "Standby! A strike is going in; a spotter round is being fired. Call it, and let us know where it goes off." Shortly thereafter the ship fired a white phosphorus round that exploded directly over the target.

Mitch and his boats were upstream from the target and our boats were downstream from it, watching the action and listening to it on the radio. Mitch came back on the radio and told our TOC, "Willie Peter [white phosphorus] on target, fire for effect!"

This was the first time my boat crews and I had ever seen a 40mm anti-aircraft gun used for an artillery ground strike. It was amazing: every third or fourth round was a tracer, easy to see at night. I was reminded of a low-arched rainbow, as the tracer rounds came up over the villages. That rainbow then "walked" its way with explosions through a wooded area near the riverbank. A few minutes later, they came back on the radio and asked, "How did it look?"

Mitch answered them and said, "It was right on target and damn, you guys are good."

After we had arrived at the pier, tied up and written up our patrol report, I went up to CIC [combat information center and chart house] to tell them how well they had done. The officer in charge said, "Thanks for the report. Nice of you to tell us. Once the round leaves the gun, we can only hope it goes where we want it to."

"You are just being modest," I said, "but please tell the gun crews we appreciate the kind of support we just witnessed."

Chapter 34
Visits to two Support Bases
Up River

Our day patrol began about 08:00, and our mission took place in the extreme northern part of our patrol sector of the Vam Co Dong River. Some important papers had to be hand-delivered to the US Army. Loading everything, we checked our fuel and ammo, then headed north. Our first stop was an army firebase just north of Ben Luc eight or nine miles up river.

Our boats turned into a small stream north of the main river, and about a half-click back we spotted their tents and compound. As our boats tied up alongside the small, make-shift US Army pier, the army troops welcomed us. A South Vietnamese army unit was encamped alongside the tented area, and it looked as though the soldiers had their families with them. A wire fence stood around the outer perimeter for protection; concertina wire and claymore mines completed the defense of the place.

I asked one of the sergeants who had greeted us, "Do you guys ever get hit?"

"About three or four times a week Charlie tries to lob mortars in on us," he replied. "Sometimes snipers take shots at us, so we have to stay on our toes."

I presented the duty officer with his package. Our payment was an invitation to lunch. It was a good visit. Besides the food, we shared information about the area and the river. One of the men said, "Man you couldn't get me on one of those little boats of yours out in that river! You're an easy target and easily hit."

I said, "We know, but we run pretty fast and hope Charlie is a bad shot." We thanked them for the hospitality and the lunch.

Returning to the main river, we continued upstream through an area called the Eagle's Beak. Previously it had been a VC and North Vietnamese staging area, where much action had taken place. The north side of the turn in the river had been bombed with heavy B52 strikes, and the wooded area was shredded, looking like craters in a plowed field with chunks of trees and limbs sticking out at strange angles. One of my men spoke up, "This must be some heavy-duty Charlie territory!"

"I heard that it was and still is. Don't let your guard down, guys, and watch both sides of the river," was my reply. We continued on up river. Beyond the point of total devastation, a small stream branched off to the south; we turned into it. About 100 yards on the right was the next outpost on our delivery route.

This was a South Vietnamese Army outpost with about twenty American Army personnel attached to it. As we approached the compound, our army counterparts came out and greeted us. The sergeant in charge said, "We stand relieved by the navy. Thanks for coming guys!"

I said, "No not this time, sarge. We've got a package for your commanding officer." He accepted it and had it sent to him.

I asked him how things were this far out and this close to Cambodia. How was it with Charlie, I wanted to know, this close to the local army and with so few men?

"Not easy," he said. If you only knew! Our South Vietnamese base commander is a 4.0 guy, but some of the others are not. We found some of the claymore mines for perimeter defense had been reversed on us and could not figure out how this could have happened. Had we command-detonated them, we would all be wiped out by now. A few days ago we turned them back and set a watch on them ourselves. A South Vietnamese executive officer turned them back on us. When he finished, we knew we were about to be hit. Yesterday our base commander called his XO out in front of us, pulled his gun and executed him with one shot to the head. Saying, "This is what I think of Cong," he pulled the trigger.

"We turned the mines back around, and we were hit last night again. Sorry. It didn't quite go the way they planned this time."

And we thought we sometimes had it tough in the river patrol force! Thanking them, we wished them luck and departed. Our run back down the river was at full speed--and was easy today. We don't think we've been fired on. Frequently the only way of knowing is a direct hit on you, or your boat. At night it is easier to detect firing. Muzzle flashes, tracers and rocket trails betray the enemy.

Chapter 35
Hutches on a Sand-Filled Swamp

Finally taking shape was our base compound, which was being pumped out of the brown water of the river. Because the landfill had thick sand in it, the pumps were now able to stop. After grading, hutches were built and a deepwater well drilled through the sand. The Seabees and construction crews were certainly not wasting any time! In just a few days they had erected several buildings. Therefore we were able to move the River Division off the cramped quarters on board ship into tin roof-covered buildings with wire screens and all-around paneling.

Our toilets were of the simplest design. A few inside portable units and the urinals were merely large pipes sticking up out of the sand. That perfectly describes the privacy we had out on the boats. Mosquito netting covered our new bunks, so we wouldn't have to slap mosquitoes all the time. It wasn't fancy, but we did have elbow room.

In our chief's hutch, there were a table, a few chairs and some portable lockers. A motor generator provided us with electricity from somewhere out on the compound. Completing the search of our new facilities, we found a radio, tuned it to the primary frequency of our boats, and never turned it off again. By leaving the radio on all the time, we could, in chief's quarters, hear what was happening and who on the river was in trouble. So that nobody would be tempted to transmit on it, the chief had removed the microphone.

Chapter 36
Night Patrol and
Friendly Chopper Fire

All good things must come to an end, they say. Again, my crews and I had night patrol scheduled. Our briefing officer informed us we would be setting bank ambush near the army firebase north of Nha Be, not far from Eagle's Beak. He said to be aware that intelligence was predicting tonight up to forty VC and North Vietnamese regular army soldiers would try to cross at that point.

"What a comforting thought," one of my boat captains said.

"Be on the north bank, and once they commit to crossing, you know what to do-- so good luck, guys," the briefing officer said.

We briefed our crews, made sure the boats were ready, tightened our flak jackets, made sure our helmets fit and then went on our way. As planned, we arrived on location just after dark and set up in the edge of the nipa palm. Camouflaging our boats, we gazed at the clear sky and bright moon. Our location was about 300 yards south of the little stream leading to the army firebase that we had visited a few days earlier. When we were fully set up, I coded up our co-ordinates, called them into our TOC, and asked them to caution the firebase of our position. "Please don't shoot us," were our words; "we're out here on the river." Not long after the request, the firebase contacted us on our secondary frequency, acknowledging that our presence was known.

Our senses were tuned and ready, lookouts were in place, and our starlight scope was in hand--but there were no VC in sight. After we had been sitting there a few hours, two helicopter gunships flew up river from us and started using their mini-guns on our riverbank. It was saturation firing, and headed our way! My first reflex was to get us out into the river and to make sure our flag was flying. Maybe the trigger-happy fellows would see us in time-- even in the moonlight! So I said in a voice so loud that our cover boat could hear it without the radio, "Let's get out of here out into the river!" As we tried to clear, one round from the sky hit the deck about three inches from my foot. My cover boat also received one round hit, but fortunately no one was hurt. After seeing us move out into the river, they ceased fire. Apparently they recognized our profiles or saw our flags. After discussing it with our TOC, we were for calling off the mission at that point. But the boss said no.

Resetting in-bank ambush, we also quietly reset the watch. What was that sound about ninety minutes later? As we sat in silence, still nervous from the friendly fire near miss, three or four mortar rounds went off barely 100 yards inland from our position. The rounds fell onto the fire base compound. Quickly I called in to our TOC, which gave me permission to contact the army post directly. Establishing contact, we informed them of our location and where the rounds had originated. When I reported our coordinates, I, of course, compromised our position--but it had to be done. "Thanks Shapeless Two Zero," was the response. "Please move to a safe distance upstream for a few minutes. Say when clear, over."

Our response was, "Roger that." We broke ambush and went upstream a few hundred yards past the stream leading back to their compound, again blending in with the bank. We are clear to the north, was my next transmission. Within fifteen seconds a blanket of airburst shells saturated the area of the mortars with shrapnel.

We are finished. Thanks again, guys," they said a couple of minutes later.

After that, we called it off. Apparently there was too much activity on our side of the river for Charlie to come across tonight. What the enemy had seen surely caused him to decide not to move. Since it was a long way home, we wrapped it up and departed.

Chapter 37
Death of a Friend

My first day off the river in a while was supposed to be quiet. I planned nothing beyond relaxing and writing an evening letter home. After lunch Mitch Wells and Everett Collier asked me if I would like to play some cards with the other guys in their living quarters. Sure I said. There were six of us around the table playing penny poker, dime limit, just passing the time of day, enjoying the company and telling sea yarns about our patrols. Everyone at that poker table had had a number of firefights.

Around 15:00 Signalman First Class Howard Maner remarked, "It was fun guys, but I have to finish this and get my patrol ready for the river." For some time now he had been patrol officer for boats #23 and 24. "See you guys," he said cheerfully.

Mitch Wells said, "Watch yourself out there."

Maner responded with, "I will." As he left, he threw up his hand to all in a cordial gesture of farewell.

We continued to play cards for another hour or so and the game broke up. Soon we went our separate ways. About an hour later word spread quickly through the compound that Maner's patrol had been hit and that there were casualties. Several of us gathered for information in the division commander's office. The division CO came in, cleared his throat awkwardly, and announced in a low voice, "Sorry guys, but Maner took three rounds in the back and is dead. No-one else on his boats was hurt to the best of our knowledge."

We stood around in the office, discussing the tragedy. He left behind a wife and five children to whom he was very close. Then the division CO spoke up, "This is hard to do. But I need to ask for a volunteer to take over his patrol tonight."

I spoke up first, saying, "You have one. He was my friend and it's the least I can do for him right now. If it's all right with you, sir, where he got hit is where I would like to set up. Maybe we can catch them!"

He said, "You got it."

Within the hour, his boats and I were back on the river just north of Ben Luc where he had been hit. Ben Luc was a village southwest of Saigon on the Vam Co Dong River. As we patrolled and searched the night, nothing happened--and no one was spotted. Since we were so angry with the enemy, it was in the interest of hostile forces to remain hidden from us. As the night passed, the VC fired not a single shot--nor did we. Frustrated that we couldn't find the killer, we returned about 04:00 we returned to base empty-handed.

Next day we had a memorial service for our slain friend. All who were not on active duty on the river attended. He was a good man, a friend to all of us and popular among those in the river division. Praying for his family, we took comfort from the belief that our dead comrade was now in God's safe keeping.

A day or so later, a lieutenant commander from one of the units upstream was visiting our compound on business. He had lunch with us and was saying how difficult it was to work with some of the Vietnamese in his compound. He said it was like trying to bring a sixteenth-century people into the twentieth century. But we had to do it, he reasoned, so that we could go home someday and let them defend themselves.

As he said good-by, we saluted him and wished him luck. Then he boarded his boat and headed somewhere north. About an hour or so later, the Seawolf gunships were called in for a strike at the Eagle's Beak in the river. As chance would have it, the lieutenant commander's boats were passing through the area that had been previously pounded by B-52 Bombers. All at once his boat was hit by rockets and automatic weapons' fire. Several of the men were hurt. As for the LCDR himself, sad to say that he took a rocket and was lost over the side of the boat in the explosion. Another good man lost. When will it all end?

The lieutenant commander didn't belong to our river division, but it was widely known that he was one of the finest navy officers who had ever served in this war-torn country. He was well liked and respected by all those who had worked with him and who had had only the briefest acquaintanceship with him.

Chapter 38
Night Ambush from Point-Blank Range

My night patrol was quickly approaching. Our area of patrol was just north of Ben Luc, where Maner's patrol had been hit. When darkness began to set in, we rounded the bend in the river and eased into a bank near where several old bunkers had been blown up during previous raids. Although the nipa palm along the riverbank was kind of thin and didn't offer much protection, each boat found a bunch to tie up to. When all light had faded into the west, we turned the radio down low and waited silently.

Others, we knew, monitored our radio frequency, so we had to be careful about our every single word. The South Vietnamese outpost in the bend of the river about a quarter mile downstream fired a few rounds, some carrying in our direction. Since we never let them know where we were going on the river at night, they may not even have known we were there. Around 21:30, a Vietnamese voice came on our radio in a hushed tone in English saying, "Some Americans are going to die on the river tonight." That announcement sent chills up our backs.

We stayed on alert, and as the night wore on, serious fatigue set in. In spite of exhaustion, we tried to remain vigilant. All of us, I'm sure, were in a state of half sleep by 01:30. All at once my senses returned to 100% awake and aware. Without making a sound, I stepped up on the engine cover behind the M60, thumbed the safety off, and listened. Something was moving in our direction as quietly as possible. My instincts were not to make a sound, not even to the crew. All at once a man stepped from behind a patch of nipa palm about fifteen feet away. He opened fire at the same time I did with about a ten-shot burst. I hit my target. As he fell, a bullet passed very close to my face. When they heard this exchange, our forward .50s' gunners on both boats started firing vigorously.

"Hold your fire," I yelled loud enough for everyone to hear. When they stopped firing, the footfall of someone else running away was audible. We put in a few more bursts in his direction with the .50s and M60, while our boat captain tossed a couple of grenades as far as he possibly could. As we pulled out of ambush and headed south, we wondered if this was the same assassin who had killed Maner.

Chapter 39
Airborne Mud Jump

The Army 101st Airborne had some troops working in the area, and our next patrol involved them. When we went to briefing, the 1st Lieutenant and Sergeant with the 101st were present. They planned to conduct a night operation about a hundred yards from the river on the bank of a small stream. There a couple of our patrols had had contact with sampan gunrunners a few nights earlier. So we loaded them up, about seven or eight to each boat, and headed north. As we approached the insertion point, the sergeant pointed to where he wanted to be dropped off. While our cover boat stood guard for us, we nosed into the bank. As the airborne guys moved away, a few of them eased over the bow into the swampy water with mud up to their ankles.

Thereupon, one of their squad decided he was going to show the navy how the army disembarked a boat on a mission. So here he was, full pack, M16 at the port arms position, and announcing in a strong voice, "Airborne," as he jumped into the mud. What a shame! He sank into mud and water halfway between his knees and butt. Looking back at the sergeant, Mr. Airborne didn't say a word, for he was stuck.

The sergeant inquired, "Chief, you have a rope; do we need to pull this airborne idiot out?"

Of course, we tossed him a line and pulled him out. He was for sure embarrassed, and all of us had a chuckle out of the situation. As they disembarked, we wished them luck. The following evening we would return and pick them up.

They had contact that night with someone trying to throw grenades into their night camp. However, the assault was foiled just as a VC was about to toss his first grenade. Our guys sighted and destroyed one sampan, but the occupants stole away into the night.

Chapter 40
Operation Caesar II

Enemy activity was increasing in our patrol sectors. More often we were working with the American army, navy SEALS and others. At this morning's briefing, we learned that several of our riverboats will provide a blocking force so the army can make a sweep on the south side of the river. We're part of a massive operation called Caesar II. In conjunction with us, American forces north of Ben Luc are sweeping toward the river in search of the VC and NVA [North Vietnamese Army]. More than a hundred US soldiers of several squads will try to flush out the enemy. If our adversaries attempt to cross the river, I feel certain they'll be "ours."

Command has restricted our firing to defense with small arms and grenades, because the .50s could easily carry into friendly positions. Accordingly, we spaced our boats out and patrolled the river with good vigilance. Not much was happening, so we eased into the south bank near some scattered nipa palm and other brush. Here we could observe the river without being seen ourselves. We sat there awhile. Late in the afternoon, as we monitored the radio and any activity on the river, we heard gunfire several hundred yards inland from us. It sounded like M16s and AK47s. Be alert, guys! Something is happening back there, I informed our crew. Nervously we sat there watching and listening for any movement. A short while later we heard a thrashing, running sound about 150 feet away, coming straight for us. I yelled, "Identify yourself! Are you American?"

The noise stopped, no answer, I repeated my words, adding this time in my best Vietnamese the phrase Chu Hoi Phycom." Still no answer. Then it started again, sounding like two or three bulls loping through the underbrush toward us. "Get us out of here," was my command to both boats. As the coxswains started the boats and slammed the throttles in reverse, my boat captain and I pulled the pins on frag grenades and tossed them in the direction of the sounds. As the grenades exploded, there was still no answer or sight of anyone. Twice we asked them to identify themselves. But they never did.

Our blocking force patrols continued in the area. The operation was to last several days around the clock; we could leave only when relieved by another patrol on station. Into the second day the activity on the river was light-- no sampans to speak of. As the sun was setting and the light fading into the west, our boats were at the north end of our assigned patrol area. My bow gunner yelled out, "Chief, look!" He was pointing at a sampan crossing the river from north to south with five hard-rowing passengers in it. As fast as we could, we turned and headed in their direction. Before we could intercept them, they entered a small feeder stream. I picked up a flare and was about to ignite it over the stream, when a burst of automatic weapons' fire came from there. A round hit the flare in my right hand, igniting it and burning my arm. But I felt fortunate to have escaped with a minor wound.

Stunned, and temporarily blinded by the flash, my crews saw what had happened and fired a few bursts from our M16s and M79 grenade launchers. It took a few minutes for my eyesight and other senses to return. In a higher state of alert, we remained on patrol. Charlie, trying to evade the sweep, had only sporadic contact with our other patrols.

Around midnight we were relieved and went back to the boat dock. I had the duty corpsman put some salve on my burned arm and then hit the sack.

Next morning, as we were about to have breakfast, one of the patrol officers came up to me. He wondered whether I had heard what had happened last night after our patrols had left the river. "No, what?" was my reply.

Everett Collier sat down with me and said, "Jim, you know the army guys we've been supporting?"

"Yeah," I said.

"Well five of them were killed last night on the south side of the river while they were encamping under a tree. Charlie had set up on them because they had bivouacked there the night before. From what we were told, our boys were getting comfortable for the night and Charlie fired rockets at the tree. The rockets exploded on impact and the shrapnel got them. A big loss in American lives," he said.

Chapter 41
Enemy Fire from
Friendly Positions

The blocking force for Operation Caesar II continued into the third day. This cordon-and-search operation, made in conjunction with the US 199th Light Infantry Brigade, was to last a full eight days. Early in the day my patrols went out to relieve the night crews. Today the 101st Airborne operation on the north side of the river spotted a large number of VC and North Vietnamese regular army troops. They had been terrorizing the locals, South Vietnamese civilians.

As we tightened up our patrols on the river, the American Army started driving the enemy toward us. The whole operation was about 1½ miles up river north of Ben Luc. Suddenly my boats began receiving automatic weapons' fire from five or six positions on the northerly bank line. Realizing that the American forces were close to them, I called our cover boat. "Two Zero Alpha, this is Shapeless Two Zero," I called out. "As you can see, we are receiving fire from the north bank. Do not, repeat, do not return fire! Move your unit as far from the fire as possible! They're trying to draw our fire into our own people, over."

"Roger, Two Zero," they came back, as both boats increased their distance from the deadly incoming rounds.

One of our radios was tuned to the same frequency as the ground command troops. Establishing contact with them, I shouted, "This is Shapeless Two Zero. We're receiving small arms' fire from the north bank near a thick cluster of nipa palm. Because friendlies are too close, we are not, repeat not, returning fire, over."

"Roger, understood," was the reply of the ground radio operator.

A booming voice came over the radio, demanding to

know: "Shapeless Two Zero, are you in those little boats down there on the river?"

"That's affirmative," was my answer. "To whom am I speaking, over."

"I'm in orbit above you, son. Thanks for not firing on my troops! Stand back and watch. Stay over there where you are!"

"Roger," was my reply.

Another voice came on the radio, "Shapeless Two Zero, we're monitoring your situation. Give me the grid coordinates you're receiving fire from." I acknowledged, giving our exact location. Within minutes, two F-100 fighter-bombers made a strafing run with 20mm cannons that shut the firing down. The planes made two more passes about 550 meters inland from the river, firing their guns and dropping four bombs. As the bombs burst, trees and debris scattered into the air over 200 feet high.

One of our boat crew said, "Man, that is awesome! I'm glad those guys are not coming after us! This is just like in the movies."

As the fighting subsided, air strikes and artillery were called off. The army made its sweep, discovering twelve dead men with weapons where the first strafing run had been made. A few hundred meters farther inland the sweep produced a large cache of weapons and over thirty additional enemy casualties. Most of the dead were soldiers in the North Vietnamese regular army.

Our flag was flying clear in the slight breeze. As if to salute it, the light observation helicopter that had hovered over the area during much of the fighting came in flying mighty low over the river near our boats. The now familiar strong voice came back on the radio: "Shapeless Two Zero, we want to thank you and all of you men on the river for your help in making this a successful operation, over."

"You are welcome, sir, anytime. Thanks, and the best of luck," was my answer. I watched him lift up over the treetops and head towards the southeast.

Chapter 42
Interrogation of a VC

After my patrol had ended and the night was near, I wandered down to a ship at anchor. Since it was scheduled to depart the area soon, I knew this was the right time to say good-by to a few friends on board. Entering the ship, I made my way up to the chart house. Then I heard some commotion in the pilothouse, where an ARVN soldier stood over a Viet Cong prisoner. The VC lay on the deck, hands and feet tightly bound. During questioning, his hands and feet were pulled up hard against his back. An American civilian, apparently not of the Brown Water Navy, seemed disturbed by my presence. "We're interrogating a prisoner, Chief, please leave us."

My response was a quiet and surprised, "Yes," as I looked back at the bloody man on the floor near death.

Not what I had expected to see on board! Wondering when, if ever, this cursed war would end, I departed ship and went back to our hutch up on the compound. Now the thoughts that I had suppressed came forth fully. Interrogating prisoners was indeed a necessary part of war. But of all the talents at my command, questioning captives was not one of them. The danger was, of course, that the need for survival could cause people to go too far. I could still see the bloody man in my mind's eye.

Chapter 43
A Bad Grenade Kills
One of Our Own

Sometimes the heat in Vietnam got extreme. Humidity wasn't the only problem, however. The blazing sun affected any metal that was exposed to it, including hand grenades. Grenades in prolonged heat, we were told repeatedly by command, were unstable, and therefore dangerous to our boat crews. We were to dispose of any "hot" grenades.

One of our boat captains (not of my boats) got the idea to rid himself of his overheated grenades while his boat was tied up to the pier. One afternoon he started pulling the pins on some and tossing them into the river. They exploded underwater, killing fish--one of our methods for catching them, by the way. The water was about 20 feet deep alongside our floating pier. Pulling the pin on one grenade, the captain saw it explode as it left his hand. The concussion hurled him over the side into the water. An immediate search began. But we weren't able to locate the captain, who was probably not alive. The swift current forced us to extend the search far downstream. Many boat crews looked for his body--and failed. Finally, the search was called off, and the captain was considered missing--and presumed dead.

Four days later my patrol was operating downstream about four miles from the pier. As we scanned the banks for enemy activity with binoculars, I spotted a strange target. A body, tangled in nipa palm, was floating by the edge of the bank. I could see his green pants and combat boots. Face down in the water, he wore no shirt. Good lord, it was BM2 Minsey, our missing boat captain! Our relief at finding him was decidedly mixed, for we still had to recover our dead comrade. What if, instead, our efforts caused the body to sink? That was the very worry of my boat captain, who suggested that I take the wheel and hand him the boat hook. Meanwhile I had contacted our base TOC and reported we had found the missing accident victim. The irony didn't escape me that, even in the middle of a rescue, we needed to keep watching our own backs.

Since we were not equipped for body retrieval, we inquired whether any other boats were in the area. Two RAG boats were on their way up river to lend assistance and bring him home to rest. A few minutes later they pulled in behind us with their dreaded cargo. I could clearly see a body bag, fully realizing what it was for. Now we were hunting not for the VC, but for a corpse. As we eased in closer to the bank, the forward gunner excitedly announced, "Fresh footprints in the mud on the bank, Chief!"

"Be alert guys! Watch out for snipers and booby traps," were my words to everyone, including our cover boat. We managed to pull the drowned man out far enough from the water to get him into the body bag. Somehow I took comfort from the fact that the water was not able to lay claim to him. Then the RAG boat crews carried him to the base. Thanking them for their efforts, we continued our patrol.

On the opposite side of the river we sighted three men carrying a long silvery object. They were too far away for a positive identification, however, so we settled for reporting it.

Chapter 44
VN Outpost Night Attack and a Crossfire Gauntlet

Our briefing prior to patrol informs us we'll be going down river again tonight. This time we're heading for the lower section of our patrol sector near a South Vietnamese outpost. It is our choice where to set up in order to monitor the river.

While the crews were loading the boats and getting ready for our night patrol, I spotted a bucket of M16 ammunition loose rounds and a couple of empty clips on the pier. Wonder who left this ammo behind? In the bucket were tracer rounds, so I filled both clips with nothing but tracers. On board we had a roll of duct tape, allowing me to tape both clips together, back-to-back. Next, as we left the pier heading south, I loaded the clips in one of our M16s and set it down near me. Although we expected enemy activity tonight, just as we did on every patrol, there was no special intelligence confirming it.

About an hour before dark, we pulled into the small stream on the south side of the main river where the outpost was located. Turning our boats around, with the bow towards the main river that was about 200 yards away, we tied up to a small pier. Shortly thereafter, a visitor appeared.

An American Army sergeant came down and said, "Hi guys. It's sure good to see some Americans for a change!"

"Hello Sarge, what's the army doing this far out?" I asked. We introduced ourselves, showing our boats to him and the VN soldier at his side. Small talk clarified our reasons for being on the river.

"Up in the compound we have a people-sniffer radar run up on a pole. It's intended to keep an eye out for what's around us. There are also rubber-duck listening devices out in the river in several places," he said with pride. "Would you like to take a look?" he wondered.

We accepted his offer, one of my boat captains and I accompanying them. But before leaving, our cover boat captain was assigned to watch the boats and send a runner, if we were needed. Seven men remained on the boats. Walking up the hill about a hundred yards to his office in the compound, he inquired about our plans for tonight. On one of his charts, I pointed to the spot where we were planning to set up an in-bank ambush after dark.

"Good," he observed. "That's only about half a mile up river from here. And before you go in, we can give you a reading on the area to make sure it's clear of enemy forces."

"That's some equipment you have there," I remarked.

"It reads body temperatures and compares them to the surrounding areas. You better believe it's accurate! If this thing says something is there, it most likely is," he explained.

"How many American troops are assigned to the compound?" I wanted to know.

"There are only three of us here. The South Vietnamese treat us very well. You couldn't ask for better people to work with," he claimed, as he showed us around the compound.

We thanked him for the tour, wished him luck and bade him farewell. Walking back to the boats, I noticed there was still some daylight left. Since it was unwise to go to our night positions while there was light enough for Charlie to see us, the men waited at the pier until sunset. I told both crews to relax a little while. About 20 minutes later, as darkness fell, we were about to cast off our lines and get underway when gunfire erupted from the other side of the compound. My sharp command was, "Hold it! Let's see what is happening before we leave. We may well have to evacuate these guys." The gunfire increased. I yelled to both boat crews, "Helmets on, flack jackets secure, everyone get down! Fire only if fired on, watch the stream behind us and the banks across from us! It appears the compound is being hit from the other side." The fighting was very intense for about ten minutes, tracer rounds whirring close over our boats.

Then my radio came on with, "Shapeless Two Zero! Why are you attacking that outpost?" The voice belonged to my division commander.

My response was, "This is Two Zero. We're not attacking the compound. We are tied up to their pier, protecting them from the south and southeast, and standing by for evacuation of friendly forces, if needed. They are being attacked from their west with automatic weapons' fire and explosions of some type, over."

"Have you fired your weapons?" he asked urgently.

"Negative," was my reply. "They were being hit from their west-side. It was my decision to remain here, provide support, protect their east-side, and render assistance if needed, over."

"Good! Stay there until this settles down," he came back, obviously relieved that we had not yet attacked the compound.

"Roger, understood," I said to him.

Helicopter gunships were called in to make several strikes on the attackers with mini-guns and rockets. After the area was clear, the army firebase at Tan An put in an artillery strike on the far side of the compound--the origin of the attack. After 20 minutes of quiet sitting in the open, my crews and I felt like exposed targets. By about 21:45 we were growing more and more uncomfortable. Just as we were preparing to get underway again, the army sergeant came running down the hill with his hand in the air. Attempting to prevent our departure, he raced up to our lead boat.

"Glad I caught you before you left," he exclaimed. "Thanks for standing by as a safety valve and covering our backs for us! Your division commander called and told me you were still here. Sorry! We thought your boats were somehow involved when the firing started. Remember where you showed me on the chart that you'd be setting up in ambush tonight? Don't do it! Your boats will sail right into a trap. Three men are exactly where you thought they'd be, so be aware! Expect to get hit when you go through there!"

"Thanks," was my reply. "Did the compound suffer

much damage, and are your men all O.K. after the attack?"

"This time we all managed to survive. We were damn lucky," he said.

We wished him and his men continued good luck and personal safety. Next I informed our boat captains and crews to be on full alert and, once we got out there, to fire at anything that fired on us first. "Let's hit the river running as hard as we can," I shouted. "Stay tight!" was my command to our cover boat captain. Both boats entered the main stream of the Vam Co Dong with throttles full open, and then we turned, heading north.

My eyes were fixed to the port side. While I studied the riverbank, stealing a glance at the radar, our cover boat opened fire at the bank to our starboard. At least fifteen muzzle flashes and a couple of rockets were aimed at us. "Fire!" I yelled to our boat crew. But the men were already a step ahead of me. The crews were firing into the muzzle flashes along the bank to our right. Due to recoils from all the firing, the steering of the boat had become difficult. To compensate, the boat captain took special pains to gain control and to drive a straight line. Then our boat engineer took a bullet in his left leg.

He yelled, "Chief, I'm hit!"

I quickly looked and yelled above the gunfire, "Can you drive?"

"Yes," he yelled back.

"Take the wheel," was my reply. I put my hand on the boat captain's shoulder and told him to take the 60.

He said "O.K." and then swapped places. In the effort to suppress the incoming fire, every weapon was still firing to our starboard side. Besides watching radar, I kept my eyes on the cover boat about thirty feet behind us.

The M16 with the tracers was in my left hand, as I bellowed into the radio handset that we were under attack. I gave our location and requested Seawolf support, because we were running a long gauntlet of automatic weapons and rocket fire. The TOC acknowledged the call.

We neared the spot at which the army sergeant had said

we would be hit. Sure enough, three automatic weapons started firing at us. Caught in the crossfire, I flipped the safety off the M16 and began firing, walking every round toward the firing muzzle flashes. I continued firing away until the clip was empty. At last the fire was extinguished. Meanwhile, army forces back inland beyond the tree line spotted our .50 cal. tracers. Thinking they were under attack, the soldiers returned fire.

Our TOC came back on the radio and said that the Seawolves were already committed to another mission, so air support was not available. Having just cleared the kill zone, we were able to stop firing. The guns were white hot, the rounds in the chambers cooking off. [The heat of the firing chamber causes the rounds to fire.] For safety's sake, ammunition had to be removed from the .50s and M60s.

One man was hurt with a bullet through his left leg, a clean wound. Another sailor on our cover boat was wounded in his right hand. Several bullets pierced each boat, but thankfully all the rockets fired at us missed, although some not by much. We returned to the pier at our base compound on the river. Medical personnel were standing by on the pier when we arrived to remove, and care for, our wounded. None of the wounds was life threatening. Both men had indeed been very fortunate.

We were all extremely lucky tonight, I told our crews. I could not compliment them sufficiently for the fine job they had done. Tonight they had shown themselves to be professionals in battle; this night they were truly men of valor. After debriefing and writing up the action, we called it a night.

The fight was monitored on the radio by the other chiefs in our CPO hutch. "What happened?" they demanded. "You guys had the world lit up down there tonight!"

My response was, "Please try to avoid cross-firefights, guys. They effect the nerves, especially after they're over."

Map 3

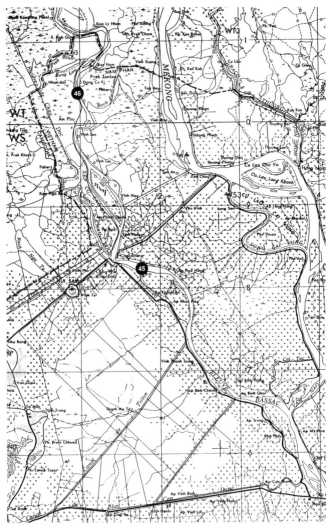

Chapter 45
Taking on Vietnamese Crews and the Move to Chau Duc

All things had to end, and that included all-American crews in River Division 591. We were moving again, this time over to the Hau Giang River, where we were to take on, and train, part- Vietnamese crews to be boat captains. Our living quarters were re-locating to the middle of the river, up near Chau Duc, very close to the Cambodian border. Stoically, we made preparations for the move.

Within a week we were all set. We packed everything and headed to our new home. It turned out to be a large anchored barge, floating in the middle of the river with some living quarters, offices and other support units built onto it. Alongside the large ammi-barge was, sitting lower in the water, a smaller barge that contained a repair shop for our river boat repairs.

After we got settled in, our patrols began again. They were quite different from the previous ones. The river was much wider. No way that our Vietnamese counterparts wanted to go into any kill zones, especially at night. So we had to monitor river traffic, passing out Chu-hoi leaflets to influence the enemy to turn himself in to us or the South Vietnamese authorities for protection. We offered a reward for information. Very few takers, none on my patrols at least. During the day it wasn't too bad.

Chapter 46
Night Patrol Near An Phu

Briefed before night patrol, we were told to check out the northern sector up near An Phu. "Activity may be detected, so stay alert," was the word. Our patrol ventured up near the Cambodian border. Our boats had two ARVN soldiers each, as trainees. When informed where we were going, they protested vehemently, "No! Too much VC up there! No can go." On my boat one of them curled up inside the bow that was referred to as chief's quarters, while the other cowered in the corner close by the grenade locker. We continued on up river.

It was about 21:00 when we arrived at our location. Having informed our operations center of our coordinates, we were to remain in the area and not go north of the island in the river. No doubt: We were very close to Cambodia.

Soon thereafter, artillery rounds started falling about 1500 meters upstream in a wooded area off to our right. I told my boat captain, "You know that stuff is falling in Cambodia, don't you?" On the radio again, this time I informed our TOC, "The strike is falling out of our grid square, over."

Their reply was, "Disregard what you are not seeing, repeat not seeing! Do you understand, over?"

"Roger, affirmative," was my answer. As we drifted down river, we saw a few muzzle flashes from the bank off to our starboard side. But we didn't return fire, instead moving our boats out of their effective range. Had we opened fire in return, many of the villagers behind them would have been killed or hurt by our weapons. I didn't want that. No boats were spotted coming out of the bordering country. When our patrol ended, we returned to our floating home.

Chapter 47

I'm Hurt, and It's Time to go Home

My time to rotate out and go back home was drawing near. Hard to believe, but my tour was almost up. My river division commander sent for me. When I arrived at his office, he said, "Chief, I am taking you off the river because there are only a few days until you're shipped out."

Only two words escaped from my mouth, "Thank you." My duties were to assist new crews in assignments, orientation-- and just about anything else that was necessary. After living in the middle of the river for a few weeks, I was ready. Boy, was I ready!

Six days before transfer date, our division yeoman and I were standing, talking, between the gangway leading down to our repair barge and the boat repair shop. About three feet separated the gangway and the shop. On the periphery of my vision, I caught sight of a small replenishment ship, proceeding upstream. The water was swift, maybe five or six knots. Abruptly, and without warning, the boat, caught in the speeding current, lost control and slammed into the ammi pontoon barge. The captain had been attempting to turn around upstream to come alongside, when he lost it. At the ferocious impact, the gangway started closing in on us, and as I shoved our yeoman out of the way, I realized that it was too late for me. I got caught across the mid-section with the gangway, as it was closing, pinning and crushing me. Now the pressure forced the air from my lungs, and I let loose with shrill sounds. A couple of the guys saw what was happening and jerked the bottom of the gangway from its brackets and off of me. All I could think was: It's almost time to go home, and now I have to go and get hurt! All my strength was gone, as I lay helpless on the deck. The doctor and corpsmen were quick to my side. Placing me on a stretcher, they carried me to sick bay.

The doctor x-rayed me and said, "No broken bones, Chief, but we don't know what else may be wrong inside. We'll keep you and pull blood every few minutes to check your white cell count. How much pain are you in?"

"I have no strength left, a sick feeling across my whole gut, and my shoulder hurts bad," I told him.

About 09:00 the doctor came in again and said, "Chief, the last blood sample indicates your insides are all torn up. Your white cells are rising fast. We'll medivac you out; the chopper's already been called." Several of the men from the division came to see me and to wish me well, which meant a lot to me. One of my boat captains said he would include one of the boat's flags in my personal possessions, soon to be packed. I thanked him with all the energy I could muster.

In less than fifteen minutes, I was loaded aboard a helicopter and strapped into a seat. I wasn't feeling well at all. Shortly we were underway to an army hospital somewhere south of where we had been. About fifteen or so minutes later we landed and were met by a group of medical personnel. Having been briefed about my condition, they took me into their field hospital emergency room, drew some blood and took another x-ray.

The blood workup came back shortly, along with the x-ray. The doctor said, "You have internal bleeding, Chief. We'll need to go in and fix it."

By this time I was about out of it. The last thing I recall was counting backwards from a hundred: 100, 99, 98--and that was it.

I woke up alongside the nurse's station with a foot-long bandage on my stomach. I still wasn't feeling any better. Gradually I could make out IVs in both arms and a tube sticking out of my left side through a large cut that was only partially sutured up. The doctor came in as I was awakening.

"We had to take out your ruptured spleen, about half of your pancreas and a badly bruised part of your liver. Hope we got everything! It was quite a mess in there."

A few hours later a low grade fever started, and my white cell count started racing up again. By the time the doctor arrived, my head was arched back and my throat was emitting deep gurgles. Blackness surrounded me. Then I entered a dark tunnel at whose opposite end, at an angle of about 45 degrees, a clean, very bright light emerged. Moving closer to it, I heard the doctor say, "We've got him back! Prep for surgery; he's bleeding internally." Then I saw it again. Once more I perceived a dark tunnel, and I was moving slowly toward the white light. But this time, when I came back to consciousness, the doctor was up on the gurney, straddling my stomach, hitting me in the chest and pumping my heart with both hands.

I remember groaning, "Oh, that hurt!"

"Hold on, Chief," he urged. "We're almost there." Then there was a dash for the ER. A cover went over my face--and off to sleep again.

Next time I woke up I was back in intensive care, with an old army sergeant standing over me. "You almost bought the farm boy," he announced. The doctor came back in shortly after I woke up.

"Glad to see you're awake! That was a close one. Your spleen stump was bleeding, and we had to repair it because a suture had come loose. We'll watch you closely because you are not yet out of the woods. You needed several pints of blood," he said.

"Thanks," I replied.

After a few days I told the medic at the desk near me, that I needed to let my wife know what has happened to me.

"Sure," he said. He sent someone in to me with writing paper and pen. Someone else gathered information so my family could be notified. I managed to scratch out the words of a letter home, saying I had been hurt and was in an army medivac hospital. But I did stretch the truth: Not to worry! I would be delayed in getting home, but everything would turn out O.K.

But then my fever returned and my white blood count

started to climb again. "What now?" Was my question to the medic who brought me the unwelcome news.

Two doctors came in to see me. One said, "You're developing an infection, and something else is wrong in there-- we don't know what, There's no choice but to go back in."

I made some dumb remark like, "Maybe you could put a zipper in for me."

The doctors laughed it off. When the lights went out this time, three of them were standing over me.

Back in ICU again and awake. This time something else was protruding from my right side. As I grew more coherent, two of the doctors came in. One said, "We think everything is fixed. You had a cracked, or leaking intestine that caused your internal problems. And your large scar down the front had some infected tissue removed from it. You'll have to wear this colostomy on your right side for a few months until the healing process on the inside is completed."

The days passed slowly, the monsoon rains came. During the downpour I thought of home. The steady pounding of the rains on the tin-covered Quonset hut they called a field hospital reminded me of the tin-covered barns down home in a rainstorm. I wrote home again, feeling a little better than before. A few more days passed. An old sergeant was looking after me, keeping me company from his nearby desk. When he wasn't too busy we talked some. I clearly recall that he constantly offered me words of encouragement. "Take your medicine, do what the doctors say, and you'll get better!"

All at once he stood up, snapped to attention, and threw a sharp salute to an officer walking up to his desk. "Good morning, Sergeant. At ease," the high official said, as he returned the salute. "Do you have a Chief Bryant in here?"

"Yes sir, right here," as he stretched his hand toward me.

I looked over and tried to move. "Admiral Zumwalt, was all I could say."

"Don't try to get up, Chief. I hear you had a pretty rough time of it."

"Yes sir, but I do hope the worst is behind me now."

He put his hand on my left arm and said, "You will pull out of this, Chief. You've done a good job for me and the Navy. When you get back home and request your next assignment, use my name to help you get it. If that doesn't work, contact me personally."

My reply was, "Thank you, sir, for coming, and I will definitely do that."

The admiral shook my hand and said, "Get well, Chief, we need you!" Then he turned and left.

It made me feel good that the Chief of Naval Forces in Vietnam would take the time to look me up and wish me well.

The days passed very slowly and the rains continued. But finally the skies cleared up. My health seemed to follow the weather. My strength was slowly returning and I wanted to go home. Every letter home told my family how much I missed everyone. As soon as my recovery was well underway--in spite of all those tubes and bandages attached to me-- my mind began to dwell on the home front. Would my wife, daughter and son still love me after a year's absence? When my wife and I said good-by in San Diego before this thing began, my body was healthy. But now it's gone through some pretty heavy trauma, including three, and possibly more, surgeries. My weight has dropped considerably, and it shows. Will I be accepted back, as if nothing had happened? And what will I do if they don't want me again? My wife was writing to me every week, sometimes a lot more often. For my part, I wrote as often in return. But much had changed. My heart was heavy.

After about a month of lying on my back in the US Army's 29th Evac. Hospital in Vietnam, recovering, eating solid food again and having some of the tubes removed, the doctor came in. "Chief," he told me, "I think you're getting well enough to travel. So if we can get this low grade fever down a little more, we're going to send you on a medivac flight to Japan-- and from there home.

"Thanks for everything, Doctor, because I really want

to get out of here and go home," I told him.

The next day the last of the tubes were removed except a small drain line in my left side taped firmly in place. I was given instructions on how to care for my colostomy. They brought in a litter to carry me into the plane. Since I had been walking around some, building my strength back, I had wanted to walk, but the docs said "no." The old army sergeant who had been caring for me wouldn't accept a mere handshake good-by. He hugged me and said, "Good-by, Chief, you've been a good patient, served well and have friends in high places. So best of luck to you and a full recovery. God bless you." We waved to each other as they hauled me out the door.

The flight to Japan was uneventful. About fifteen of us were on stretchers, some in worse shape than I. I kept thinking: we're on our way out of the war zone and going home. Touching down in Yokosuka, Japan, we were transported to the Naval Hospital for tests, evaluation, and further transfer. After checking me over, the doctors determined I should remain there a few days before being sent home. They hooked me back up to an IV, but allowed me to push it around on a roller rack.

My first thoughts were of a telephone call home. The operator placed a call for me. It was tearful and heartwarming. My wife had not been contacted by anyone about my injuries except through my letters to her, and many questions remained. "They'll be sending me on my way in a few days," I tried to reassure her.

After almost a week there, I got up, walked around regularly, and had all the tubes removed, including the drain hole tube in the left side. I was ready to go home. The doctors cleared me for the next medivac flight to Portsmouth, Virginia.

Several of us were being shipped out the same day. We were taken to a medivac plane specifically set up to carry ambulatory patients. It was a small flying hospital with a doctor and nurses ready to respond to any problems. Even though we all had to remain in bed for the entire flight, we didn't really mind. The important thing was that we were going home.

The plane landed in Norfolk, Virginia, and eight of us were taken by ambulance bus to the Portsmouth Naval hospital. Immediately the doctors checked us over and assigned us a ward. We arrived at the hospital around 10:00, still early in the day.

When everything settled down after checkout, I put a question to the doctor: "When can I go home? I live in Virginia Beach."

"Sorry Chief, but we have to keep you overnight before allowing you to go home," he said.

"Doctor, I just spent over a year away from my family. I don't plan to wait any longer, and I certainly am going home tonight. I've never been AWOL in my entire navy career, but unless you authorize me to go, tonight I will be."

"O.K.," he said, "but get the hospital ward number and check in with them, if any problems develop. Be back here at 0900 sharp."

"Thank you doctor, was my reply," as I shook his hand.

My phone call home was brief: "Honey, I am at the Portsmouth Naval Hospital in the recovery ward on the second floor. Could you bring me something to wear home?"

About an hour later I was walking up the corridor in my hospital pajamas and housecoat, feeling stooped over and thin. Walking toward me was a beautiful woman, who got off the elevator with a bag of clothing in her hand. As we neared each other she said, "Hi honey, welcome home." I choked up, tears coming to my eyes. I was home.

Nha Be "Game Warden" Base, Republic of Vietnam, June 1967. (U.S. Naval Historical Center Photograph)

EPILOG

This is a true account of my tour with the River Patrol Force, Division 591 in the Republic of Vietnam in 1968 and 1969. It is one man's opinion and viewpoint, but based on Patrol Operations Statistics that I maintained from the River War.

Jimmy R. Bryant
SMC, USN, Ret.
70% Disabled Veteran

REPORT
9 Jan. '69

Re: Bryant, SMC (Patrol Officer)

While on a routine night patrol on Long Tau River, the patrol officer and I popped flares to light up a stream where possible enemy contact had been sighted on radar. As the flares started to light up the area we came under heavy rocket and automatic weapons fire of approximately 800 meters in length. The Patrol Officer and I were blown to the after portion of the boat by the first rocket blast. Even while trying to get back to the radios to report this attack he directed us to open fire and stood clearly exposed to enemy fire to direct the first return fire from our guns, before calling for assistance. This clearly helped in the first few seconds as everyone was in a dazed condition from an exploding rocket and did not clearly realize the exact area the attack came from. This clearly showed the Patrol Officer's determination to do his job even though under heavy fire.

R. Stark
Engineman First Class
Boat Capt.

Two of our supporting Seawolf helicopters and the *U.S. Harnett County* at anchor south of Ben Luc. One gunship takes off on a strike mission against the Viet Cong. (Photo by John W. Fletcher, JOSN, USN)

Glossary

ARL
Light Repair Ship

ARTY
Artillery

ARVN
Army, Republic of Vietnam

ASPB
Assault Support Patrol Boat

BC
Body count

Black Ponies
OV-10A Bronco aircraft

CAS
Casualties

CCB
Command Communications
Boat

CINCPAC
Commander in Chief, Pacific

CNO
Chief of Naval Operations

CONUS
Continental USA

DMZ
Demilitarized Zone

DD
Destroyer

DE
Destroyer Escort

EOD
Explosive Ordinance Unit

KIA
Killed in action

LAW
Long Range Anti-Tank
Weapons

LCPL
Landing Craft, Personnel, Large

LCU
Landing Craft, Utility

LHFT
Light helicopter-firing team

LRRPs
Long Range Reconnaissance
Patrol

LSM
Landing Ship Medium

LST
Landing Ship Tank

MSL
Minesweeper, Light

MSM
Minesweeper, Medium

NVA
North Vietnamese Army

Pat. Off.
Patrol Officer

PBR
Patrol Boat, River

PCF
Patrol Craft, Fast

PG
Patrol Gunboat

PRU
Provincial Reconnaissance Unit

RAG
River Assault Group

RF/PF
Regional Forces/Popular
Forces

RPG
Rocket propelled grenade

SEAL
Sea, Air, Land (USN Special
Warfare Personnel)

SKIMMER
Small two man boat

TOC
Tactical Operations Center

USA
United States Army

USN
United States Navy

USS
United States Ship

VC
Viet Cong

VNMC
Vietnamese Marine Corps

VNN
Vietnamese Navy

WIA
Wounded in action

WBA
Waterborne ambush

WPA
Patrol Boat (USCG)

YTB
Large Harbor Tug

Patrol Operations Reports

The following logs are copies of the actual Patrol Operations Statistics reports during 1968 and 1969. The original copies were printed in old blue mimeograph copy and have faded with the passing of time. Many of them were enhanced with a #2 pencil so the pages would be legible enough to copy. No changes have been made to any of them. Many of the records did not survive but these that did offer an overview of part of the operations of River Division 591 and some of the other River Divisions we worked closely with.

Report logs…

DATE/TIME	BOAT(S)	ACTION

012330H JAN 69 WHALER LTJG SHANNON, EN1 LANE, EN2 HUTCHISON, SET UP BANKSIDE AMBUSH AT YS017732. HEARD MOVEMENT; NEG CONTACT.

031525A JAN 58/80 ABHC FAUGHT, PAT OFF, OBSERVED 2 RKTS FIRED AT S.S. OVERSEAS ROSE. PBR'S RETURNED AND SURPRESSED FIRE.

032200H JAN WHALER LTJG BECK, EN1 LANE, EN2 HUTCHISON, SET UP BANKSIDE AMBUSH AT YS113705. OBSERVED MAN WATCHING POSITION. TOOK UNDER FIRE. 1 KIA PROB. BROKE AMBUSH WITHOUT FURTHER CONTACT.

060815H JAN 27/134 TM1 WARD, PART OFF, SUPPORTED EOD CHECKING JUNK SUNK BY AUSTRAILIANS AT YS220739.

080252H JAN 27/134 QMC STPHAN, PAT OFF, OBSERVED VN LCU UNDER ATTACK AT YS013675 WITH 5 B-40S (2 HITS). PBRS AND LCU SUPPRESSED FIRE. WHEN RETURNING TO HOME BASE TO REARM 5 SAMPANS WERE SIGHTED AT YS020764. UNABLE TO PURSUE DUE TO LACK OF AMMO.

071100H JAN 23/23/58/80 LT MCGHEE / BMC COLLIER, PAT OFF, SUPPORTED COMMANDO INSERTION AND SWEEP OF AREA WEST OF CAN GIO. COMMANDOS SIGHTED 6 VC IN 24 HRS PERIOD TOOK UNDER FIRE RESULTS UNK.

071905H JAN 25/26 BM1 MEDLEY, PAT OFF, INSERTED AND SUPPORTED 8 PRUS AT YS167909. NEG CONTACT.

082242H JAN   58/80   SMC BRYANT, PAT OFF, POPED 2 FLARES AT XS984785. AS FLARES ILLUM, BEGAN RECEIVING HEAVY A/W FIRE FROM 10 - 15 POSITION AND 5 OR MORE ROCKETS, 72 BOAT RECEIVED ONE ROCKET HIT IN BOW. 4 US WIA (SLIGHT). PBR'S SUPPRESSED FIRE.

101930H JAN   58/80   ASHC FAUGHT PAT OFF, INSERTED AND SUPPORTED 8 PRU' AT YSO87555. NEG CONTACT.

120827 JAN   58/80   LTJG SHANNON PAT OFF, PROVIDED BLOCKING FORCE AT YS017765 FOR SUPPORT OF OPERATIONS IN CONJUNCTION WITH ATTACK ON MSTS SHIP LINFIELD VICTORY.

141520H JAN   25/26   LTJG BECK, PAT, OFF, OBSERVED A/W FIRE DIRECTED AT SAMPANS IN VICINITY OF XS980776. AREA WAS SWEPT WITH NEG CASUALTIES, NEG RESULTS.

141800H JAN   WHALER   LTJG SHANNON, EN1 LANE, GMG3 ROUSE SET UP BANKSIDE AMBUSH AL XS987787. OBSERVED MOVEMENT ON NORTH BANK OF STREAM., SAW 2 PERSONNEL AND TOOK THEM UNDER FIRE, RECEIVED ONE GRENADE THROWN FROM SOUTH BANK. OBSERVED ONE MAN ON SOUTH BANK TOOK UNDER FIRE. BROKE AMBUSH AND WAS TAKEN UNDER FIRE FROM 2 A/W POSITIONS OF SOUTH BANK. SUPPRESSED FIRE AND CALLED IN ARTILLERY. RESULTS 2 VC.KIA (BC) I VC KIA (PROB).

152007H JAN   25/26   LT MCGHEE PAT OFF, OBSERVED SAMPAN EVADING INTO STREAM AT XS 984763. RECONNED AREA, RESULTS UNK.

152335H JAN   25/26   LT MCGHEE, PAT OFF., COVER BOAT IN VIC XS993765 HEARD VOICES. LEAD BOAT CONDUCTED PSYOPS SPEAKER MISSION AT XS998785. LEAD BOAT RECEIVED TWO RPG RDS FROM XS984784. LEAD BOAT BEACHED AT XS950798 DUE TO POSSIBILITY OF SINKING. COVER BOAT RECEIVED 2 RPG RDS ALSO BUT BOTH MISSED. RESULTS 5 US WIA (3 RETURNED TO CONUS).

19/72 LTJG SHANNON PAT OFF PROCEEDED TO ASSIST LT MCGHEE AND SUPRESSID FIRE WHILE IN ROUTE.RESULTS UNK.

171941H JAN   23/24   BMC COLLIER PAT OFF, SUPPORTED PRU ELEMENT THAT MADE CONTACT WITH 2 SAMPANS. AT XS997787. THEY LET THE FIRST PASS AND TOOK THE SECOND WITH 5 VC ABOARD, UNDER FIRE AND CALLED FOR EXTRACTION. PBR'S PROCEEDED TO EXTRACT AND TOOK I SAMPAN WITH 2 VC ABOARD UNDER FIRE AND FOUND AN OBJECT APPROX. 6' X 18" WHICH WAS LATER IDENTIFIED AS A [500#] MINE. PBRS EXTRACTED AND REINSERTED PRUS. PBRS AGAIN EXTRACTED PRUS, RETURNED TO NHA BE AND PICKED UP EOD AND MORE PRUS. PBRS THEN RETURNED TO AREA WITH AIR COVER AND

TOWED MINE TO NHA BE WHERE EOD ATTEMPTED TO DISARM IT AND IT EXPLODED. RESULTS 7 VC (BC) (5 BY PROS, 2 BY PBR). 3 PERSONNEL FROM THIS DIVISION SUFFERED BROKEN EAR DRUMS FROM MINE EXPLOSION AND WERE SENT TO CONUS.

180726H JAN   18/72   LTJG BECK, PAT OFF, INSERTED PBRS FOR SWEEP OF AREA AT XS998787. NEG CONTACT.

202000H JAN   58/80   ABHC FAUGHT, PAT OFF, INSERTED AND SUPPORT ED 8 NHA BE PRUS AT YS132519. CONTACT MADE WITH 3 PERSONS IN SAMPAN BY PRUS. TAKEN UNDER FIRE EVADED TO WOODS. PRUS EXTRACTED AND PERSONNEL WERE CAPTURED BY PBRS. NEG CASUALTIES.

210102H JAN   25/26   LTJG SHANNON , PAT OFF, HEARD NOISES GENERATED BY METAL CONTACTING METAL, RECONNED BY FIRE. RESULTS I SECONDARY EXPLOSION AT YS180708.

221140H JAN   58/80/27/134/25/26   LT DECLERCQ, LTJG BECK LTJG SHANNON, PAT OFFS, SUPPORTED SWEEP AND NIGHT AMBUSH POSITION OF CAN GIO COMMANDOS AT YS183760, NEG CONTACT. SWEEP YIELDED 3 MILITARY STRUCTURES DESTROYED, I SAMPAN CAPTURED.

242345 JAN 23/24/80/58   BMC COLLIER, ABHC FAUGHT, PAT OFF, MSF SET UP AT YS033754. TOOK I SAMPAN UNDER FIRE WITH 3 VC KIA (PROB). PBRS CONDUCT ED FALSE EXTRACTION

252226H JAN   19/72   SMC BRYANT, PAT OFF, SUPPORTED MSF AT YS028796 WHO MADE CONTACT WITH 2 SAMPANS PBRS FROM THIS UNIT AND TWO FROM RIVER DIVISION 592 PROCEEDED TO AREA TO MOVE AMBUSH ACROSS RIVER. RESULTS 2 SAMPANS DESTROYED 6 VC KIA (PROB).

261114H JAN   27/134   LTJG BECK PAT OFF, CONDUCTED 4 BOAT RECOVERY MISSION WITH UNIT FROM 594. CAME UNDER FIRE FROM YS038789 WITH 4 RPG ROUNDS AND 3 A/W POSITIONS. PBRS SURPRESSED FIRE. NEG CASUALTIES. PROCEEDED NORTH., FOUND, AND RETURNED TO NHA BE, WITH SAMPAN FROM YS026797. RETURNED TO SUPPORT MSF IN CONTACT. SET UP BLOCKING FORCE AT YS037780. RESULTS UNK.

251405H JAN   19/72/58/80   SMC BRYANT, ABHC FAUGHT, PAT OFF, S.S. ROYAL VENTURE UNDER RPG ATTACK FROM YS010. VN RAG AND 4 PBRS RECONNED AREA. RESULTS UXK.

281300H JAN   19/72   SMC BRYANT. PAT OFF , NV RF CO 601 SAW ONE RPG FIRED AT DAI DUNG FROM VIC. YS046735 PBR'S HEARD 5 EXPLOSIONS, PBR RECONNED AREA. RESULTS UNK.

290154H JAN 25/26 BM1 MEDLEY PAT OFF INSERTED AND SUPPORTED 8 PRUS AT' XS983557. EXTRACT WITH NEG CONTACT.

011928H FEB 27/134/19/72 LTJG SHANNON/SMC BRYANT, PAT. OFFICER, PROCEEDING TO SET UP 4 BOAT BANKSIDE AMBUSH CAME UNDER ENEMY ROCKET AND AUTOMATIC WEAPONS FIRE FROM BOTH BANKS OF TAC ONG TRUN, COORD YS122741 TO YS119740. ALL FOUR BOATS RETURNED AND SUPPRESSED FIRE. TWO RKTS HIT ONE BOAT INJURING ONE MAN, SEAWOLVES, SPOOKY AND FIXED WING STRIKES WERE PLACED IN AREA. A TOTAL OF 13 ROCKETS WERE FIRED AND 25 AUTOMATIC WEAPONS POSITIONS OBSERVED. RESULTS: 1 USN WIA (SLIGHT), ENEMY-UNK.

020210H FEB 27/134/23/24 LTJG SHANNON/BMC COLLIER, PAT. OFFICER, SET UP FOUR BOAT BANKSIDE AMBUSH ON UPPER GO GIA & THI VAI. ONE SAMPAN OBSERVED MOVING SOUTH & WEST ON SMALL CANAL. SAMPAN EVADED INTO NIPPA PALM. AREA RECONNED. UNKNOWN RESULTS.

031955H FEB 23/24 BMC COLLIER, PAT. OFFICER, INSERTED SEALS AT XS983782, SEALS PATROLED 100 METERS, OBSERVED FOUR FIGURES MOVING TOWARD THEM. TOOK UNDER FIRE. RECEIVED RETURN FIRE AND SUPPRESSED, HEARD MORE MOVEMENT. CALLED FOR EXTRACTION DUE TO LOW AMMO. LHFT PUT STRIKE IN AREA. RESULTS: 3 VC KIA(BC); 1 VC KIA(PROB).

051400H-060500H FEB 25/26/27/134 LTJG SHANNON/LTJG BECK, PAT. OFFICER, INSERTED PRU UNIT AT XS997787. SIX HOURS LATER EXTRACTED FIRST UNIT, INSERTED SECOND AND SET UP NIGHT AMBUSH. NEG RESULTS.

072300H FEB 27/134 LTJG BECK, PAT. OFFICER, PSYOPS TAPE MISSION XS962803 & XS983784. PUT SPEAKER IN ANCHORED SAMPAN.

101847H FEB 27/134 LTJG BECK, PAT. OFFICER, AFTER PBR'S FROM 592 AMBUSHED ON TAC ONG TRUN, PROCEEDED TO RENDER ASSISTANCE TO BEACHED PBR. PROVIDED COVER ALL NIGHT. ALSO PROVIDED COMMUNICATION RELAY FOR MSF-5.

58/80 ABHC FAUGHT, PAT. OFFICERS, ESCORTED LCU'S TO BEACHED PBR TO ATTEMPTED SALVAGE. PROVIDED COVER FOR OPERATION.

121959H FEB 25/26 LTJG SHANNON, PAT. OFFICER, RECONNED 4 LIGHTS ON BEACH AT YS017670. RESULTS UNK.

182202H FEB 23/24 BM1 MEDLEY, PAT. OFFICER,

SIGHTED 3 MEN ON EASTERN BANK OF LONG TAU AT YSO36702. TOOK UNDER FIRE. RESULTS UNKNOWN.

230951H FEB   19/72   SMC   BRYANT,   PAT.   OFFICER, SHIPPING ATTACK ON USNS OCALA VICTORY AT XS990763. TWO RPG ROUNDS SHOT, BOTH MISSED, RECONNED AND SUPPRESSED FIRE. SEAWOLF & ARTY CALLED IN. RESULTS UNKNOWN.

230850H FEB   19/72   SMC   BRYANT,   PAT.   OFFICER, SIGHTED U/W EXPLOSION AT YSO25745. 300 FT. WATER GYSER ABOUT 150 FEET IN DIA. NEG CASUALTIES.

221900H FEB   27/134   TM1 WARD, PAT OFFICER, INSERTED PRUS AT YS004564. EXTRACTED. NEG CONTACT.

240134H FEB   23/24 BMC COLLIER, PAT. OFFICER, INSERTED PRUS AT YS004564. EXTRACTED. NEG. CONTACT.

242315H FEB   19/72   LTJG   SHANNON,   PAT.   OFFICER, HEARD HEAVY MOVEMENT FROM NUMEROUS POSITIONS ON BOTH BANKS GO GIA. RECONNED AREA. RECEIVED SMALL ARMS FIRE FROM YS178710. SUPPRESSED AND OBSERVED SECONDARY. NEG CASUALTIES. RESULTS UNKNOWN.

26193H FEB 23/24   LT DECLERCQ, PAT. OFICER, INSERTED PRUS AT YS076762 AND YS117722. EXTRACTED. NEG CONTACT.

271358H FEB   58/80   ABHC FAUGHT, PAT. OFFICER, 6 ROCKETS FIRED AT S.S. LAWRENCE VICTORY GOING SOUTH ON LONG TAU AT YS038648. NO HITS. IMMEDIATELY RECONNED AREA AND CALLED IN ALHFT. RESULTS UNKNOWN.

271950H FEB   25/26   LTJG BECK, PAT. OFFICER, INSERTED PRUS AT YS064774 AND EXTRACTED. SET UP PBR AMBUSH AT YS038761 AND YS030763. NEG CONTACT.

281242H FEB   58/80 LTJG SHANNON PAT. OFFICER, WHILE ON SPECIAL MISSION ON LONG TAU OBSERVED RUSTY CYLINDRICAL OBJECT ON BEACH AT YS013684. INVESTIGATED AND FOUND 122MM ROCKET MOTOR AND 1 TRASH CAN WARHEAD. TURNED OVER TO VNN.

020301-020832H MAR.   58/80   ABHC   FAUGHT,   PAT. OFF., INSERTED SIX RSSZ PRUS AT 020301H. TM1 WARD PAT. OFF., EXTRACTED AT 020832. NEG. CONTACT, REG, RESULTS, NEG CAS.

040020H MAR.   27/134   TM1 WARD, PAT. OFF., SIGHTED SAMPAN GOING INTO SMALL STREAM, RECONNED AREA WITH 40MM. RESULTS UNK.

040850-041700H MAR.   25/26   LT . DECLERCQ, PAT. OFF., INSERTED PRUS AT T5024656 AT 040350H AND EXTRACTED AT 041700H. RESULTS NEG.

051800-052100H MAR.   25/26   BM1 MEDLEY, PAT. OFF., INSERTED PRUS AT YS018733 AT 051800H. WHILE STANDING BY AS SUPPORT STA. PBR'S SIGHTED LIGHT AT YS015758 AT 051945. RECONNED AREA, LIGHT DISAPPEARED. PROCEEDING SOUTH, BOATS RECEIVED AK-47 FIRE AT YS013748 AT 052026H. RECONNED WITH 40MM. AT THE SAME TIME PRUS CAME INTO CONTACT AT YS018733 RECEIVING SMALL ARMS AND B-40'S FROM ALL DIRECTIONS, PBR'S SCRAMBLED TO THE SCENE RECONNING TO THE PRUS RIGHT FLANK ALLOWING THEN TO ESCAPE NORTH. PBR'S RECEIVED 4 B-40'S, SMALL ARMS FIRE, AND TWO FLARES, PRUS WERE SUCCESSFULLY EXTRACTED AT YS018733 AT 052031H. LHFT AND FIXED WING A/C MADE STRIKES IN THE AREA. FRIENDLY CAS: 1 VN WIA, I USA WIA, FM. CAS.: UNK.

060120-060145H MAR.   25/26   BM1 MEDLEY, PAT. OFF., DURING ROUTINE LONG TAU PATROL., BOATS SIGHTED LIGHT AT Y5046717.   VN   COUNTERPARTS   NEGATED   CLEARANCE   AS FRIENDLIES WERE CLOSE BY AND HAD VN PBRS INVEST. FARTHER. FOLLOWING INVEST. CLEARANCE WAS GRANTED AND U.S. AND VN PBR'S RECONNED THE AREA TO EAST AND WEST SUSPECTING IT MAY BE A VC CROSSING AREA. RESULTS: UNK.

060622-060700H MAR.   25/26   BM1 MEDLEY, PAT. OFF., AT 060622H PBR'S ON LONG TAU PATROL RECEIVED TWO RDS. OF SNIPER FIRE FROM YS015748. THE PBR'S RECONNED THE AREA WITH 50CAL AND 7,62 FIRE. ON THE SECOND FIRING RUN AT 060635H PBR'S RECEIVED A/W FIRE AT YS013749. PBR'S SUPPRESSED THE FIRE, NAVY LHFT SENT TO PROVIDE OVERHEAD COVER. AT 060651H LHFT PLACED H&I STRIKE AT YSO14747. PBR'S RECEIVED SNIPER FIRE FROM WEST BANK OF LONG TAU VIC. YS015748 AS THEY WERE RETURNING TO NHA BE.

071830H MAR.   58/80   LTJG SHANNON, PAT. OFF., SIGHTED BUNKERS ENROUTE STATION AND DESTROYED SAME.

090900H MAR.   58/80   ABHC FAUGHT, PAT. OFF., SIGHTED OBJECT AT YS009683 AND PROCEEDED TO INVEST. FOUND A RUSTY 122 ROCKET MOTOR, FITTED WITH OVERSIZE 122 WARHEAD FITTINGS AND ONE FRAG GREN. BLEW GRENADE, TURNED MOTOR OVER TO VN AUTH. AT NBA BE.

092016-100212H MAR.   23/24   LTJG BECK, PAT. CFF., 092016H INSERTED PRUS AT YS033749. AND YS036749 EXTRACTED, NEG. CONTACT, NEG, RESULTS.

112020H MAR. 25/26 BM1 MEDLEY, PAT. OFF., (UNITS FROM OTHER DIV. ALSO INVOLVED) AT YS112020H DURING SEAL INSERTIONS HEARD VOICES IMMEDIATELY AHEAD OF INSERTION CRAFT. TWO VC SIGHTED AND TAKEN UNDER FIRE. SEAL CRAFT EXTRACTED, RCVD. A/W FIRE XS983785 AND XS984786 AT THE SAME TIME PBR'S RCVD. THREE B-40'S FROM XS984783 AND A/W FIRE FROM XS981799. PBR'S RETURNED FIRE. 591 UNITS ASSUMED POSITIONS IN AREA, SAW LIGHTS ON THE BANK AND TOOK UNDER FIRE. LHFT PROVIDING OVHD. COVER.

111905H MAR. 58/80 ABHC FAUGHT, PAT. OFF., SIGHTED EVADING SAMPAN, FIRED WARNING SHOTS SAMPAN DISAPPEARED INTO SMALL CANAL IN A RESTRICTED AREA. LHFT PLACED STRIKE IN UPPER END OF SMALL CANAL TO DRIVE SAMPAN OUT. NEG. RESULTS.

110445H MAR. 25/19 LTJG SHANNON, PAT. OFF., FIRED H&I INTO SUSPECTED ENEMY AREA. RESULTS UNK.

101904-110152H MAR. 25/19 LTJG SHANNON, PAT. OFF., INSERTED PRUS AT YSO85752. NEG. CONTACT. NEG RESULTS, PBR'S STOOD BY AT VIC YS120725 AND SUCCESSFULLY EXTRACTED PRUS AT YS085752 AT 110152H.

150010H MAR. 23/24 SM1 MANER, PAT. OFF., PBR'S DRIFTING IN MIDDLE OF THI VAI WITH ENGINES AT IDLE RECEIVED ONE B-40 AND A/W FIRE FROM VIC YS203670. PBR'S IMMEDIATELY SUPPRESSED FIRE AND RECONNED AREA. RSLTS UNK.

182104-190223H MAR. 19/72/27/134 SMC BRYANT AND GMGC WELLS, PAT. OFFS., INSERTED PRUS AT XS814670 AND XS833689. AT 190215H ONE TEAM MADE CONTACT WITH FIVE VC IN A SAMPAN AT XS814672. RESULTS: 4 VC KIA(BC), 1 VC WIA, CAPTURED. ONE AK-47 AND ONE AK-50, DESTROYED 30 MINES, CAPTURED VARIOUS DOCS. PRUS EXTRACTED AT XS814670 AND XS833689.

212020H MAR. 56/78 ABHC FAUGHT, PAT. OFF., WHILE PROCEEDING SOUTH ON THE VAM CO DONG. RIVER, PATROL RECEIVED ONE B-40 FROM EAST BANK AT XS640700. RATURNED FIRE AND MADE ONE FIRING RUN. 2030 CALLED IN ARTY. ABOUT THIRTY SECONDS BEFORE ROCKET WAS FIRED OBSERVED A WHITE STAR CLUSTER ABOUT 500 METES INLAND.

220415H MAR. 56/40 ABHC FAUGHT, PAT. OFF., UNITS IN WBA DETECTED SAMPAN WITH ONE OCCUPANT PROCEEDING SOUTH ALONG EAST BANK VIC XS718620. PBR'S ILLUMINATED FROM WEST BANK AND OCCUPANT EVADED. UNITS DESTROYED SAMPAN.

232112H MAR.   T-112-4/T-112-8   LTJG BECK, PAT. OFF., WHILE PROCEEDING NORTH ON ROUTINE PATROL.. UNITS RECEIVED TWO B-40'S FROM XS627715 AT 232112H. UNITS RETURNED FIRE AND CONTINUED NORTH, AT XS627720 UNITS RECEIVED A THIRD RPG. ALL THREE RPG'S MISSED AND THERE WERE NO FRIENDLY CASUALTIES. ARTY DID NOT RESPOND DUE TO PROXIMITY OF POPULATION.

240002-240245H MAR.   ????   LTJG BECK, DURING ATTACK ON USS HARNETT COUNTY SCRAMBLED BOATS ALONGSIDE AND PROVIDED BLOCKING FORCE.

260353-260546H 23/24/153/25   LT DECLERCQ AND LTJG SHANNON, PAT. OFF'S, DURING ATTACK ON ARVN DREDGE DEFENSE FORCES UNITS EVACUATED 10 ARVN WOUNDED AND ALSO FERRIED TROOPS,

260042H MAR.   27/134   GMGC WELLS, PAT. OFF., UNITS IN WBA DETECTED SAMPAN WITH ONE OCCUPANT ALONG EAST BANK AT XS717656. WHEN ILLUMINATED SAMPAN EVADED INTO SMALL CANAL, COVER BOAT TOOK UNDER FIRE WITH UNKNOWN RESULTS.

260042H MAR.   27/134   GMGC WELLS, PAT. OFF., UNITS IN WBA DETECTED SAMPAN WITH ONE OCCUPANT ALONG EAST BANK AT XS717656. WHEN ILLUMINATED SAMPAN EVADED INTO SMALL CANAL. COVER BOAT TOOK UNDER FIRE WITH UNKNOWN RESULTS.

260120H MAR.   19/72 SMC BRYANT, PAT. OFF.. WUNITE IN WBA DETECTED THREE VC IN BRUSH ATTEMPTING TO SNEAK UP ON LEADBOAT. BOTH BOATS TOOK UNDER FIRE WHEN TEN METERS FROM PATROL AND BROKE AMBUSH. 3 VC KIA(PROB).

281230H MAR.   25/153   LTJG BRAY, PAT. OFF., UNITS SENT TO ASSIST 194.9.1 UNITS WHO HAD RECEIVED A/W AND SMALL ARMS FIRE AT XS660683,. NEG. RESULTS.

280944H MAR.   19/72   SMC BRYANT, PAT. OFF., UNITS RECEIVED A/W FIRE FROM XS660684 TO XS633706. FIRE WAS RETURNED AND THEN CHECKED WHEN FRIENDLIES REPORTED BEING IN THE AREA BY 5/60. UPON FURTHER CHECKING IT WAS DISCOVERED THAT ENEMY INITIATED ACTION BY FIRING ON ARMY AND NAVY UNITS SIMULTANEOUSLY. 2 WIA SLIGHT.

281304H MAR.   23   LT. DECLERCQ, PAT. OFF., SCRAMBLED ONE VN ASPB AND ONE PBR TO INVESTIGATE SWIMMER REPORTED BY BRIDGE SENTRY. NEG. RESULTS.

270400-270430H MAR.   25/153/23/24   LTJG BRAY AND SM1 MANER, PAT. OFF'S., SUPPORTED 10 TROOPS OF 5/60/9 ACTING AS A REACTION FORCE. NEG. CONTACT.

272005H MAR.   19/72   SIC BRYANT AND BMC LEWIS, PAT. OFF'S., UNITS IN WBA AT XS719645. OBSERVED MAN WALKING TOWARDS AMBUSH POSITION CARRYING A LONG CYLIND. OBJECT. MAN APPEARED TO SIGHT THE BOATS IN AMBUSH AND ATTEMPTED TO HIDE. TOSSED ONE FRAG. GRENADE AT HIS POSITION AND OPENED FIRE WITH M-60. BROKE AMBUSH AND RESET. ONE VC KIA(PROB).

292110H MAR.   23/24/T-112-8   LT. DSCLERCQ AND SM1 HANER, PAT. OFF'S., UNITS IN WBA AT XS715628, 713629, 717629. THE AN/PPS 5 RADAR WAS MOUNTED ON THE ATC ALONG WITH AN M-16 WITH STARLIGHT MOUNT. AT 290110H WI4 MEN WERE SEEN APPROACHING THE BOAT IN POSITION XS713629. THEY WERE ALLOWED TO APPROACH TO WITHIN FIVE YARDS OF THE POSITION AT WHICH TIME THEY WERE FIRED UPON. ONE MAN WAS OBSERVED TO FALL AND ROLL DOWN A BANK AMBUSH WAS , BROKEN AND AREA RECONNED. ONE VC KIA(BC) TWO VC KIA (PROB).

291245H MAR.   19/23/58/72/80   LT DECLERCQ AND ABHC FAUGHT, PAT. OFF., CSCRAMBLED PBR'S TO ASSIST IN EVACUATING CHOP-CHOP PARTY AND TO PROVIDE A BLOCKING FORCE FOR DREDGE DEFENSE UNITS IN CONTACT.

292100-292330H MAR.   23/24   SM1 MANER, PAT. OFF., UNITS IN WBA AT XS588790 OBSERVED TRACER TO THE SOUTH, AT 293205H HEARD SIGNALS ON THE BEACH. SIGNALS WERE STICKS BEING STRUCK TOGETHER. SIGNALS APPROACHED BOATS AND A PERSON FELL INTO THE WATER NEAR COVER BOAT. COVER BOAT TOOK AREA OF NOISE UNDER FIRE WITH M-16. UNITS BROKE AMBUSH AND PROCEDED SOUTH. AT XS574773 ONE RECOILESS ROUND DETONATED IN WATER [E]ASTERN OF LEAD BOAT. NO MUZZLE FLASH NOTED AND UNITS UNABLE TO DETERMINE FIRING POSITION. UNITS CLEARED AREA AND ARTY FIRED INTO AREA.

300700-300500H MAR.   25/153/58/80   LT DECLERCQ, LTJG BRAY, ABHC FAUGHT, PAT. OFF'S., INSERTED TWO COMPANIES OF 3/7/199 AT XS576780 AND 575780. SUPPORTED TROOPS DURING THE DAY. EXTRACTED AT XS575793 AND RETURNED TO BLB.

302130-300700H MAR.   58/80/23/24/25/153   LT. DECLERCQ, LTJG BRAY, ABHC FAUGHT, BKC LEWIS, SM1 MANER PATROL OFFICER, UNITS WERE PROVIDING BLOCKING FORCE FOR ARVN UNITS IN CONTACT XS628733 TO XS640698. CHIEF FAUGHT'S PATROL FORMED ORIG. BLOCKING FORCE, JOINED BY LTJG BRAY'S

PATROL. COMBINED UNITS MADE SEVERAL FIRING RUNS IN AREA OF SEAWOLF STRIKES. THREE FRIENDLY WIA (VN). TO 13VC KIA (BC) CAPTURED VARIOUS WEAPONS AND DOCUMENTS .

030900-031600H APRIL   HQ1211/27/134   GMGC WELLS, PAT. OFF., UNITS LIFTED ONE PF PLATOON OF 55TH RECON COMPANY FROM BEN LUC TO LUONG HOA TO RELIEVE ON STATION PLATOON RELIEVED PLATOON LIFTED TO BEN LUC.

031738H APRIL   ABHC FAUGHT, PAT. OFF., PATROL DETECTED SAMPAN EVADING TO EAST AT XS589790, PERSONNEL IN SAMPAN OVERTURNED IT AND EVADED TO BEACH. SMALL ARMS FIRE CAUSED A MEDIUM SIZED EXPLOSION IN THE SAMPAN, BELIEVED TO BE CAUSED BY BOOBY TRAP. PATROL FIRED INTO AREA INTO WHICH PERSONNEL DISAPPEARED AND SEARCHED THE AREA. NEG. RESULTS.

041130-041720H APRIL   27/134   GMGC   WELLS,   PAT.   OFF., INSERTED SEALS AT XS594775. TOOK TWO MALES UNDER FIRE (SEALS). ONE KIA (PROB). ONE WIA. DETAINED YOUNG MALE. INTERROG. OF VILLAGERS REVEALED VC HAD MADE THEM CARRYING SUPPLIES. EXTRACTED SEALS AND RETURNED TO HOME BASE.

040515H APRIL   27/134/T-112-8   SCRAMBLED UNITS FOR AN EMERGENCY LIFT OF EIGHTY TROOPS OF 2/50/25 ARVN DIV WHO WERE REACTING TO GROUND TROOPS IN CONTACT AT XS506712 GMGC WELLS, PAT. OFF.

042150H APRIL   58/80 ABHC FAUGHT, PAT. OFF., WHILE IN WBA AT XS573778 TWO ENEMY WERE HEARD APPROACHING PBR 58. TWO FRAG GRENADES WERE THROWN IN THEIR DIRECTION OF THE SOUND.

041800-051300H APRIL T-1210/T-1211/A-5110   LTJG BECK, LTJG KHAI, PAT. OFF., INSERTED EIGHTY USA TROOPS AND 2/60/9 INF AT XS710625 AND XS743630. THE NORTHERN ELEMENT GAINED CONTACT WITH AN NVA FORCE OF UNKNOWN SIZE. ARMY SNIPERS ACCOUNTED FOR FOUR VC DIA(BC). SUBSEQUENT LHFT STRIKE AND ARTY ACCOUNT FOR OTHER TWO. A SWEEP BY USA TROOPS YIELDED BLOOD TRAILS AND 2 BAGS OF DOCUMENTS.

051900-051630H APRIL T-122-5/T-111-9, 23/24, 25/153   LT DECLERCQ, BMC LEWIS, SM1 MANER, PAT. OFF., ELEMENTS WITH COMPANY OF 5/60/9 INF EMBARKED CONDUCTED COMBINED LAND AND WATER AMBUSHES ALONG THE VAM CO DONG FROM EAST WEST GRID LINE 70 TO 62 ON BOTH BANKS. ONE PLATOON WAS DIVIDED UP ON FOUR PBR'S AND AMBUSH AT XS719635 DETECTED SEVEN PERSONS MOVING TOWARD THEIR LOCATION. MEN WERE TAKEN UNDER FIRE AND PBR MOVED SOUTH AND

DOWN FIRE DIRECTED BY ARMY AMBUSH. SWEEP OF AREA FOUND FOUR BLOOD TRAILS AND TWO BODIES. TROOPS FOUND TWO AK-47, THREE LBS OF DOC., FIVE LBS OF MEDICINE.

060330-060630H APRIL   19/72 SMC BRYANT, PAT., OFF., INSERTED SEAL TEAM AT XS709699. SEALS KILLED A VC HAMLET CHIEF AND TWO BODY GUARDS. CAPTURED TWO GRENADES, SIX BOTTLES PENICILLIN, FIFTEEN BOTTLES MEDICINE, FOUR LBS DOCS. THEN EXTRACTED.

062000H APRIL   A-111-2/A-111-3   LTJG SHANNON, PAT. OFF., WBA DETECTED TWO SAMPANS TRAVELLING ALONG WEST BANK OF THE VAM CO DONG AT XS557307, ILLUM. AND TAKEN UNDER FIRE. THREE VC DIA (BC), CAP. TWO AK-47, ONE CARTIDGE BAG, ONE RUSSIAN FLAG, 300 LBS RICE, TWO COOKING POTS, TEA, TOBACCO, CLOTHING, FOUR LBS. DOCS., SOAP, TWO FRAG GRENADES(US).

051930H APRIL   58/80 ABHC FAUGHT, PAT. OFF., SIGHTED SAMPAN WITH FOUR NEAR BANK AT XS558303 TOOK UNDER FIRE, ONE VC KIA IMMEDIATELY OTHERS JUMPED INTO THE WATER AND WERE FIRED UPON WITH M-16'S AND CONCUSSION GRENADES, KIA (PROB) CAPT., ONE AK-50, AK CLIP,CAPTURED TWO PERS, RADIO, FIVE LBS PERS GEAR, ONE LB MEDICAL SUPPLIES, WEB GEAR, ONE CHICOM GREN., ONE LB DOCS.

062145H APRIL   58/80 ABHC FAUGHT, PAT. OFF., DETECTED A SAMPAN AT XS559802. FIRED 40MM WITH UNK. RESULTS SAMPAN EVADED INTO CANAL.

062040-062300H APRIL   19/72 SMC BRYANT, PAT OFF., INSERTED TEAM AT XS559802. TEAM TOOK SIX VC UNDER FIRE KILLING ONE OF THEM, TEAM EXTRACTED, RESET ANOTHER POINT.

062040-062300H APRIL   19/72 SMC BRYANT, PAT. OFF., INSERTED SEAL TEAM AT XS709624. TEAM TOOK SIX VC UNDER FIRE KILLING ONE OF THEM, TEAM EXTRACTED, RESET ANOTHER POINT.

081935H APRIL   19/72 SMC BRYANT, PAT. OFF., SIGHTED ONE MAN COME OUT OF BUNKER AT XS633712. MAN WAS TOO FAR TO TAKE UNDER FIRE EFFECTIVELY RELOCATED BOATS DOWN STREAM AND DETECTED TWO MORE NEAR SOUTH COORD. TOOK UNDER FIRE WITH 40MM. THREE KIA(PROAB).

081800H APRIL   T-112-3/A-111-2/27   LT. DECLERCO, GMGC WELLS, PAT. OFF., PROVIDED BLOCKING FORCE TO ELEM. OF THE 5/60/9TH AT XS645692 TO XS625730. GROUND FORCES ENCOUNTERED APPOX. 75VC 44VC KIA(BC).

082345H APRIL   19/72 LTJG BECK, PAT. OFF. (CASTRO) WBA AT XS558825. DETECTED TWO APPROACHING THEIR POSITION.

PATROL FIRED SA AND THREW GRENADES AT THE ENEMY.

092345H APRIL 19/72/58/80 LTJG BECK, ABHC FAUGHT, PAT. OFF., INSERTED SEAL TEAM AT XS558815 SEALS TRIPPED BOOBY TRAP KILLING ONE AND WOUNDING THREE OTHERS. EMERGENCY EXTRACT WAS COMPLETED WITH THE AID OF ABHC FAUGHT'S PATROL WHICH WAS JUST COMING OFF PATROL. (CASTRO)

102114H APRIL 19/72 LT. DECLERCQ PAT. OFF., (CASTRO) PATROL DETECTED SAMPAN WITH FOUR MEN MOVING SOUTH AT XS575776. SAMPAN EVADED TOWARD NIPPA PALM AND WAS TAKEN UNDER FIRE BY M-16 WITH STRARLIGHT MOUNTED AT RANGE OF ABOUT 150 METERS. MAN ON STERN OF SAMPAN WAS OBSERVED BEING KNOCKED OUT OF SAMPAN THROUGH STARLIGHT. ONE VC KIA(PROB).

101740-101900H APRIL 19/72 LT. DECLERCQ PAT. OFF., (CASTRO) PROVIDED BLOCKING FORCE AT XS632718. GROUND FORCES EIGHT VC KIA(BC), TWO 57 RECOILESS RIFLES.

102300H APRIL 19/72 SMC BRYANT, PAT. OFF., WBA AT XS580768. OBSERVED ONE MAN ADVANCING TOWARD BOAT, WHEN HE WAS WITHIN TWENTY FEET OF BOAT PATROL THREW ONE FRAG. GRENADE WHICH FAILED TO EXPLODE. THEN OPENED FIRE WITH M-16 AND M-60 AND CLEARED AREA.

101900H APRIL 58/80 ABHC FAUGHT, PAT. OFF., ROUTINE PATROL SPOTTED FIFTEEN PEOPLE ON BEACH AT XS577774,WHEN THE PEOPLE SPOTTED THE PBR'S THEY TRIED TO CONCEAL THEIR POSITION AND TRIED TO EVADE TOWARDS BUNKERS. BOATS TAKEN UNDER FIRE WITH 40MM AN 60MM MORTAR. AT 101920 UNITS RECEIVED HAW AND SA FROM SAME BUNKERS. LHFT AND ARTY CALLED IN.

110100H APRIL 19/72/58/80 SMC BRYANT, ABHC FAUGHT, PAT. OFF., UNITS IN WBA AT XS575773 AND XS580768 OBSERVING AREA OF PREVIOUS CONTACT OBSERVED HEAVY MOVEMENT AT FIRST POSITION, ANT THREE VC SEEN AT SECOND POSITION 500 METERS CARRYING A CYLINDRICAL **OBJECT APPROX. 4-5 FT. LONG.** UNITS TOOK AREA UNDER FIRE, CLEARED AREA, AND CALLED IN ARTY.

122305H APRIL 58/80 ABHC FAUGHT, PAT. OFF., UNITS IN WBA AT XS574772 OBSERVED FIVE VC APPROACHING ME BOAT ON EAST BANK. TOOK S149 UNDER FIRE. BOAT REMAINED IN WBA.

121745-122000H APRIL 58/80 ABHC FAUGHT, PAT. OFF., UNITS ON ROUTINE PATROL OBSERVED TEN PERSONNEL IN FIELD ON EAST BANK AT XS575778. PERSONNEL EVADED AND WERE TAKEN UNDER FIRE. SEAWOLVES WERE CALLED IN AND RECONNED AREA OF CONTACT. UNITS SET UP WBA 70 KEEP FIELD UNDER

SURVEILLANCE. AT 122000H ONE VC ATTEMPTED TO MOVE IN ON COVER BOAT AND WAS TAKEN UNDER FIRE. TWO VC KIA(PROB).

121950H APRIL   19/72 SMC BRYANT, PAT. OFF., WBA AT IS590772 DETECTED ONE SAMPAN WITH SEVEN PEOPLE ON BOARD GROSSING FROM NORTH TO SOUTH. TOOK SAMPAN UNDER FIRE. TWO VC KIA(PROB). TWO SETS WEB GEAR, SIX FULL CLIPS AK-47 AMMO.

131910H APRIL   SKIMMER LT. DECLERCQ, EN2 HUTCHISON, BM3 RIEMAN: DETECTED SAMPAN WITH TWO MEN CROSSING THE VA14 CO DONG FROM EAST TO WEST. FIRED WARNING SHOT AND SAMPAN ATTEMPTED TO EVADE TO WEST BANK WITH OCCUPANTS JUMPING INTO THE WATER. BOTH VC WERE SUBSEQUENTLY KILLED AND SAMPAN CAPTURED. RECEIVED SA FIRE FROM THE EAST BANK. LT. DECLERCQ SLIGHTLY WOUNDED. TWO VC KIA(BC).

131945H APRIL   SKIMMER LT. DECLERCQ, EN2 HUTCHISON, BM3 RIEMAN: WHILE SPOTTING ARTILLERY INTO AREA WHERE PBR PATROL SUPPORTING SKIMMER WAS AMBUSHED FROM, DETECTED THREE PERSONNEL ON BEACH MOVING TOWARD SKIMMER. WHEN ENEMY WAS TWENTY YARDS AWAY, SKIMMER TOOK THEM UNDER FIRE BY SA AND HAND GRENADES. ONE VC KIA (PROB).

131930H APRIL   58/80 ABHC FAUGHT, PAT. OFF. , WHILE RETURNING WITH CAPTURED SAMPAN (SEE ABOVE) PATROL RECEIVED TWO B-40 AND HAW FIRE AT XS587784. ONE ROCKET EXPLODED NEAR COVER BOAT WOUNDING THE COXSWAIN. BOAT GROUNDED IN TIE NIPA PALM ON THE WEST BANK. BOAT WAS THEN BROUGHT UNDER CONTROL B: BM1 NUGENT. ARTY WAS REQUESTED. ARTY WAS SPOTTED BY THE SKIMMER. WOUNDED MAN WAS DUSTED OFF.

140010H APRIL   19/72 SMC BRYANT, PAT. OFF., UNITS IN WBA AT XS578793 SIGHTED ONE MAN SNEAKING UP ON BOATS. WHEN MAN WAS WITHIN TWENTY FIVE FT. PATROL TOSSED TWO FRAG. GRENADES ON HIM.

140135H APRIL   27/134   GMGC WIELLS, PAT, OFF., WBA AT XS563800 ILLUMINATED AND TAKEN UNDER FIRE BY FIREFLY UNITS. NEG. PERS. MAT. CASUALTY.

141110-141400H APRIL   19/72/27/134LT. DECLERCQ, GMGC WELLS, PAT. OFF., UN17S SCRAMBLED AT REQUEST OF 3/7/199TH TO LOOK FOR ONE (USA) MAN DROWNED AT XS559805. MAN SLIPP, WHILE TRYING TO RECOVER HIS WEAPON FROM THE WATER.

142105H APRIL   27/134   GMGC WELLS, PAT. OFF., UNITS IN WBA AT XS589784 DETECTED FOUR TO FIVE PERSONNEL

APPROACHING THEIR POSITION. WHEN PERSONNEL WERE WITHIN TEN FT OF BOAT, PATROL TOOK TIMM UNDER FIRE AND BROKE AMBUSH. ENEMY GAS, UNK.

150305H APRIL19/72 SMC BRYANT, PAT, OFF., UNITS IN WBA ALT XS595770 DETECTED TWO ENEMY PERSONNEL ON BEACH APPROCHING BOATS TOOK THEM UNDER FIRE AND BROKE AMBUSH, ENEMY CAS. UNK.

150240H APRIL 27/134 GMGC WELLS, PAT, OFF., UNITS IN WBA AT XS720637 HEARD PERSONNEL APPROACHING THEIR POSITION. PATROL FIRED IN DIRECTION OF SOUND AND BROKE AMBUSH, ENEMY CAS. UNK.

151830H APRIL SKIMMER LT. DECLERCQ, SMC BRYANT, PAT, OFF., EN2 HUTHISON, EN3 STANLEY, PBR PATROL SUPPORTING SKIMMER CAME UNDER B-40 AND A/W ATTACK. THREE B-40S WERE FIRED AT SECOND PBR. PBRS RETURNED FIRE AND CLEARED TO THE NORTH WHERE THEY SPOTTED ARTY. KRAMER, EN3 WIA, BURN TO RIGHT HAND.

15130H APRIL 25/153 BMC COLLIER, PAT. OFF., PATROL HAD ONE NVA CHIEU HOI ON VAM CO DONG AT XS589798. MAN WAS CARRYING ONE CHICOM GRENADE, CANTEEN AND FIRST AID KIT. MEMBER OF C18 NVA ARTILLERY UNIT WITH MISSION TO ROCKET SAIGON. HE CLAIMED HE HAD NOT EATEN IN THREE DAYS AND THAT OTHER MEMBERS WANTED TO GIVE UP BUT ARE AFRAID TO.

150900-151100H APRIL 23/24/T-111-9 BM1 PARRISH, PAT, OFF., (RIEMAN BC) SUPPORTED, EXTRACTED THIRTY TROOPS OF 3/7/199TH TO CHECK A BARREL FOUND BY THEIR UNITS THE PREVIOUS DAY AND BELIEVED TO BE A CACHE. BARREL CONTAINED WATER. XS560805.

162020H APRIL 19/72 SMC BRYANT, PAT. OFF., PATROL IN WBA AT XS608772 DETECTED THREE VC MOVING CLOSE TO THEIR POSITION AMD TOOK THEM UNDER FIRE WITH AUTOMATIC WEAPONS.

161330-161530H APRIL 23/24/27/134 GMGC WELLS, BM1 PARRISH, PAT., OFF., SCRAMBLED TWO PATROLS TO ASSIST IN THE SEARCH FOR THE BODY OF BM2 MINSEY, BOAT CAPT. OF MSM 17 WHO HAD BEEN BLOWN OVERBOARD WHILE DISPOSING OF OLD TNT ORDNANCE

160745H APRIL 23/24 BM1 PARRISH, PAT, OFF., UNITS ON ROUTINE PATROL LOCATED THE BODY OF USA PERSONNEL LOST ON 14 APRIL. COORDS. XS5778855 (RIEMAN) BOAT CAPT.)

172145H APRIL   A-111-3/A-111-2   LTJG BRAY, PAT. OFF., UNITS IN WBA DETECTED ONE PERSON ON BEACH AND TOOK UNDER FIRE. CLEARED AREA AND RESET AMBUSH. ENEMY CAS UNK. XS721646

17930H APRIL   19/72 SMC BRYANT, PAT, OFF., PATROL IN WBA AT XS573774 DETECTED TEN PERSONS WITH WEAPONS IN TREE LINE. TWO MOVED TOWARD THEN AND WERE TAKEN UNDER FIRE. OTHERS EVADED. ENEMY CAS, UNK.

172030H APRIL   23/24 SM1 MANER, PAT. OFF., INITS IN WBA AT XS558815 DETECTED TWENTY FIVE PERSONS ON BEACH. UNITS CLEARED THE AREA WHILE FIRING. UNITS RECEIVED THE ONE B-40 AND S/A FIRE IN RETURN. UNITS THEN SPOTTED ARTY INTO THE AREA.

202210H APRIL   23/24 SM1 MANER, PAT. OFF., UNITS IN WBA AT XS562889 ON EAST BANK OBSERVED FOUR VC PROCEEDING SOUTH ON WEST BANK. WHEN ENEMY WAS ACROSS FROM PBR AMBUSH SITE PBR'S TOOK THEM UNDER FIRE.

231955H APRIL   58/80 ABHC FAUGHT, PAT, OFF, IN WBA OBSERVED ONE SAMPAN WITH THREE MEN GROSSING FROM NORTH TO SOUTH SHORTLY AFTER SEEING ONE TRACER FIRED FROM DOWN RIVER., COORD. XS606774. PATROL FIRED WARNING SHOTS AND SAMPAN EVADED. WHEN SAMPAN WAS TAKEN UNDER FIRE BY PATROL, BOATS OCCUPANTS JUMPED IN WATER. ONE VC TRIED TO CAPSIZE SAMPAN WHILE HE WAS IN WATER, BUT WAS KILLED BEFORE HE SUCCEEDED. A CHICOM BACKPACK RADIO FOUND IN THE SAMPAN WAS APPARENTLY WHAT HE WAS TRYING TO JETTISON. THREE VC KIA(BC), ONE RADIO, EXTRA RADIO BATTERY, EARPHONE, TWO LBS DOCUMENTS, ONE CHICOM GRENADE.

232345H APRIL   25/153   BMC LEWIS, PAT. OFF., IN WBA AT XS592795 HEARD VC SNEAKING UP ON BOAT. ONE VC WAS OBSERVED SWIMMING IN THE WATER NEAR THE BOAT. TOOK AREA UNDER FIRE AND CLEARED TO THE SOUTH. A FIREFLY IN THE AREA OBSERVED 'THE TRACERS AND REACTED IMMEDIATELY. FIREFLY RECONNED THE AREA WITH UNK. RESULTS.

24080H APRIL   19/72 SMC BRYANT, PAT. OFF., IN AREA WHERE SAMPAN WITH THREE VC AND CHICOM RADIO WAS INTERDICTED, PATROL FOUND A SATCHEL CONTAINING THREE LBS OF DOCUMENTS, ONE CHICOM 9MM PISTOL, TWO MAPS, AND RADIO CODE TABLES.

251918H APRIL   58/80 ABHC FAUGHT, PAT. OFF., ON ROUTINE PATROL UNITS RECEIVED THREE B-40 ROCKETS AND AW FIRE FROM EAST BANK AT XS587784. PBR'S SUPPRESSED FIRE. OV-10'S

ON ROUTINE PATROL OVERHEAD REACTED IMMEDIATELY AND PUT STRIKE ON CONTACT AREA. ARTY THEN PUT ON AREA.

250800-251130H APRIL   27/134, T-112-8   GMGC WELLS, PAT. OFF., BOATS PICKED UP SEVENTY TROOPS OF THE 50/25TH ARVN AND INSERTED THEM AT XS583770. PRIOR TO INSERTION BOATS PREPPED THE AREA EXTRACTED TROOPS AT XS589790. NEG. CONTACT.

250800-251130H APRIL   27/134, T-112-8   GMGC WELLS, PAT. OFF., UNITS IN WBA AT XS599869 SIGHTED THREE VC ON BEACH ABOUT TEN METERS FROM BOAT. PATROL LOBBED GRENADE ON ENEMY'S POSITION AND TOOK THEM UNDER FIRE WITH AUTOMATIC WEAPONS, ENEMY CAS. UNK.

261908H APRIL   SKIMMER/27/134 LT. DECLERCQ, GMGC WELLS, PAT. OFF., GMG2 CASTRO, BM2 RIEMAN; SKIMMER IN AMBUSH AT XS589790 CAME UNDER HEAVY CALIBER AUTOMATIC WEAPONS FIRE FROM EAST BANK., SKIMMER SUPPRESSED FIRE WITH 90MM RECOILESS RIFLE AND AUTO WEAPONS. PBR PATROL IN SUPPORT MADE FIRING RUN. ARTY FROM BEN LUC AND THU THUA WAS SPOTTED BY SKIMMER UNTIL RELIEVED BY FAC. WHEN SKIMMER AND PBR'S CLEARED SOUTH SKIMMER WAS TAKEN UNDER FIRE BY SA FROM THE EAST BANK ONE KILOMETER SOUTH OF THE ORIGINAL AMBUSH SIGHT. PBR'S AND SKIMMER SUPPRESSED FIRE AND CLEARED THE AREA AS FAC OVERHEAD IMMEDIATELY SWITCHED ARTY TARGET TO NEW AMBUSH SITE. ENEMY CAS. UNK.

271900H APRIL   27/134/58/80   GMGC WELLS. ABHC FAUGHT, PAT. OFF., CHIEF WELLS PATROL DETECTED SAMPAN CROSSING AT XS603772. WITH EIGHT MEN IN IT. AFTER WARNING SHOTS FIRED THE VC JUMPED INTO THE WATER. WHEN PATROL ATTEMPTED TO CAPTURE SWIMMERS AND THEY WOULD NOT SURRENDER WILLINGLY, TWO PBR'S WERE SCRAMBLED TO ASSIST IN THE OPERATION. AS ENEMY BEGAN REACHING THE BANK THEY WERE KILLED WHEN CAPTURE WAS IMPOSSIBLE AND ESCAPE WAS IMMINENT. PATROL SUCCEEDED IN CAPTURING TWO VC FROM THE WATERS EDGE AND ONE WOUNDED VC FROM THE BANK. TWO VC MADE THE BEACH AND WERE TWENTY METERS INLAND WHEN THEY WERE TAKEN UNDER FIRE BY SCRAMBLED PBR'S. AT SAME TIME ONE USN WOUNDED (WILLIAMS) BY BOOBY TRAP ON BEACH AS THREE USN'S ATTEMPTED TO TAKE PRISONERS. SEAWOLVES WERE REQUESTED AND MADE FIRING RUNS. ARTY REQUESTED BUT NOT USED BECAUSE OF POPULATION DENSITY. FIVE VC KIA, THREE POW ONE OF WHOM WAS WIA. [*WILLIAMS WAS WOUNDED IN FOOT AND LEG. HE WANTED TO BE SURE HIS "BLACK BERET" WAS INCLUDED IN HIS SEA BAG – HE WAS GOING HOME.*]

270800-271500H APRIL   T-112-8/T-121-1/19/72   BMC COLLIER, SMC BRYANT, PAT. OFF., BOATS INSERTED EIGHTY TROOPS OF 4/12/199TH INF AT XS578912 AND PROVIDED BLOCKING FORCE WHILE TROOPS SWEPT THE AREA. NEG. CONTACT. TROOPS EXTRACTED AT XS553895.

280830-271500H APRIL   23/24 BM1 PARRISH, PAT. OFF., INSERTED TROOPS OF 4/12/199TH INF AT XS553812 AND PROVIDED BLOCKING FORCE DURING THE DAY AND EXTRACTED THEM AT 281430. WHILE RETURNING TROOPS TO FSB BARBARA, PATROL DETECTED TWO VC ON WEST BANK AT XS555830 CARRYING WHAT APPEARED TO BE AK-47'S., VC WERE EVADING INTO TREELINE AND PATROL TOOK THEM UNDER FIRE. EMBARKED TROOPS CALLED IN ARTY. AFTER ARTY WAS COMPLETED, TROOPS WERE INSERTED TO RECON THE AREA. FOUND TWO WHOLE BUNKERS AND SIXTEEN DESTROYED ONES. BUT NO SIGN OF THE VC.

282030H APRIL   27/134   GMGC WELLS, PAT. OFF., BOATS IN WBA DETECTED TWO VC SNEAKING UP ON BOAT. PATROL LOBBED ONE FRAG. GRENADE ON THE CLOSEST VC AND BROKE AMBUSH.

290800-291300H APRIL   19/72 SMC BRYANT, PAT. OFF., PATROL LIFTED AN EOD TEAM FROM THIRD BRIGADE/9TH AND SEC. FORCE FROM 5/60TH TO DESTORY BUNKERS ALONG THE EAST BANK FROM XS574775 TO XS590788 WHERE RECENT ENIFF HAVE OCCURED.

291045H APRIL   19/72 SMC   BRYANT,   PAT.   OFF.,   WHILE SUPPORTING TROOPS BLOWING BUNKERS, SIGHTED FOUR SAMPANS AT XS583783 CARRYING FIVE OR SIX EXTRA VN MALES TOWARD WEST BANK. BY THE TIME UNITS ARRIVE AT SCENE THE EXTRA PERSONNEL WERE GONE. ALL FOUR SAMPANS WITH 13 OCCUPANTS WERE DETAINED FOR QUESTIONING BY BEN LUC DISTRICT CHIEF. SEAWOLVES ON PATROL CHECKED AREA WITH NEG. RESULTS.

292300H APRIL   27/134   GMGC WELLS, PAT. OFF., UNITS ON ROUTINE PATROL IN AREA OF EW 72 GRID LINE RECEIVED FIVE RPG ROUNDS AND HAW FIRE. EAST BANK.

300146H APRIL   27/134   GMGC WELLS, PAT. OFF., UNITS ON ROUTINE PATROL PROCEEDING SOUTH RECEIVED TWO RPG ROUNDS AND AW FIRE. PATROL MADE FIRING RUNS AND CLEARED AREA. COORD XS702663.

022020H MAY   23/24 BM1 PARRISH, PAT. OFF., BOATS IN WBA AT XS655686 RECEIVED S/A FIRE FROM THREE PERSONS ON THE BEACH. THEY RETURNED FIRE AT CLOSE RANGE AND BROKE AMBUSH.

022150H MAY   23/24 BM1   PARRISH,   PAT.   OFF.,   UNITS

PROCEEDING NORTH AT SLOW SPEED WERE TAKEN UNDER FIRE BY S/A FROM TWO VC IN A SAMPAN ON THE WEST BANK AT XS626719. UNITS RETURNED FIRE WITH 40MM AND DESTROYED SAMPAN, KILLING ITS TWO OCCUPANTS.

032100H MAY SKIMMER LTJG BRAY, PAT. OFF., PERSONNEL IN SKIMMER OBSERVED TWO VC SNEAKING TOWARDS THEIR CRAFT. VC WERE ALLOWED TO APPROACH WITHIN 15 YARDS AT WHICH TIME THEY WERE FIRED UPON BY M-16 WITH NOD MOUNTED. UNIT THREW ON FRAG GRENADE IN AREA OF BODIES WHILE BREAKING AMBUSH. XS602771.

061815H MAY 23/24/SKIMMER LTJG SHANNON, SM1 MANER, PAT. OFF., SKIMMER FROM RIVDIV 591 PULLED OUT OF WBA AS SUPPORTING PBR'S PASSED BY HEADING NORTH. 15-20 SECONDS LATER A LARGE EXPLOSION (MORTAR SIZED) OCCURED NEAR AREA WHERE SKIMMER HAD BEEN. A PBR PATROL CREW MEMBER SAW THE EXPLOSION, IT WAS ON A SAMPAN. ANOTHER CREW MEMBER HAD SPOTTED AN UNOCCUPIED SAMPAN IN THE VICINITY BUT SEARCH AFTER EXPLOSION REVEALED NO TRACE OF SAMPAN.

072329H MAY 23/24 SM1 MANER, PAT. OFF., PATROL RETURNING FROM BLOCKING MISSION RECEIVED HEAVY A/W FIRE FROM THE SOUTH BANK AT XS095666. PATROL MADE TWO FIRING RUNS SUPPRESSING FIRE, AND THEN CLEARED TO THE NORTH. UNOBSERVED ARTILLERY WAS REQUESTED AND PUT IN.

090130-091200H 19/72/25/153/27/134/58/80 ABHC FAUGHT, BMC LEWIS, GMGC WELLS, SW BRYANT, PAT., OFF., UNITS PARTICIPATED IN A CORDON/SEARCH OPERATION WITH 5/60/9TH INF. DIV. NATIONAL POLICE AND PF/RF BEN LUC DISTRICT FORCES IN AP BA CU HAMLET, AT 090130 4 PBR'S MADE A QUICK LIFT OF A (). 5/60TH FROM NORTH BANK OF THE VAM CO DONG (XS590772) TO SOUTH BANK (XS607773) TO COMMENCE CORDON. ADDITIONAL TROOPS AIR MOBILE IN AT XS594758 AND BY ATC 'S AN XS605758. PBR IS IN AMBUSH ALONG THE NORTH BANK UNTIL FIRST LIGHT. AT 090605 ONE SAMPAN SUCCESSFULLY EVADED INTO CORDON. SNIPER FIRE DISTRACTED PBR LONG ENOUGH SO THAT SAMPAN WAS ALMOST ACROSS RIVER BEFORE DETECTED. PBR'S RECEIEVED ONE BURST OF A/W FIRE FROM WHERE SAMPAN EVADED. NO FIRE WAS RETURNED DUE TO POSITION OF FRIENDLY TROOPS. AT BA CU HAMLET HAS BEEN THE SIGHT OF FREQUENT CROSSINGS. RESULTS: ONE HOI CHANH CAPTURED THREE US CARBINES, THREE SKS, FOUR SAND BAGS OF AK-47 EXPENDED AMMO. 100 PERSONS DETAINED BY USA.

092200H MAY 58/80 ABHC FAUGHT, PAT. OFF., PATROL IN WBA AT XS671670 TOOK UNDER FIRE TWO SWIMMERS APPROACHING BOATS. NEG. RETURN FIRE RECEIVED. TWO VC KIA (PROB)

111915H MAY   58/80 ABHC FAUGHT, PAT. OFF., PATROL IN WBA AT XS669682 RECEIVED ONE BURST OF A/W FIRE OVER THEIR POSITION. UNITS REMAINED IN POSITION AND AT 2015H TWO VC WERE OBSERVED MOVING TOWARDS THE BOATS, PATROL TOOK THEM UNDER FIRE WITH M-16 AND FRAG GRENADES AT CLOSE RANGE AND CLEARED AREA. AT 2040H, WHILE PROCEEDING NORTH FROM CONTACT AREA, UNITS CAME UNDER B-40 AND A/W FIRE FROM WEST BANK AT XS640695. ONE B-40 EXPLODED IN THE WATER OFF THE BOW OF THE COVER BOAT CAUSING MINOR SHRAPNEL DAMAGE TO THE HULL. PATROL RETURNED FIRE AND SUPPORTED SAME IMMEDIATELY. UNITS CLEARED AREA TO SURVEY DAMAGE. BLACK PONY AND ARTY PUT INTO AREA.

120303-120320H MAY   58/80 ABHC FAUGHT, PAT. OFF., PATROL SCRAMBLED TO VICINITY OF XS603723 TO XS615713 TO MAKE FIRING RUNS ON SUSPECTED VC MORTAR POSITIONS FROM WHICH THE ARVN DREDGE DEFENSE FORCE HAD JUST BEEN MORTARED, MADE FIRING RUNS UNTIL ARTY AND USA LHFT COULD BE ARRANGED.

122220H MAY   27/134   GMGC WELLS, PAT. OFF., IN WBA AT XS651693 HEARD MOVEMENT ON THE BEACH. GRENADE WAS THROWN AT COVER BOAT, HITTING BOW AND BOUNCING INTO THE WATER WHERE IT EXPLODED. PATROL THEN RECEIVED A/W FIRE. BROKE AMBUSH AND MADE FIRING RUN. ON SECIOND FIRING RUN PATROL RECEIVED S/A, A/W FIRE AND (1) ROCKET. ARTY AND BLACK PONY STRIKE MADE ON THE AREA WITH UNKNOWN RESULTS.

130240H MAY   58/60 ABHC FAUGHT, PAT. OFF., PATROL IN WBA AT XS666681 RECEIVED SHORT BURST OF A/W FIRE AND TWO GRENADES FROM EAST BANK. GRENADES FELL SHORT IN WATER ASIDE COVER BOAT. UNITS TOOK AREA UNDER FIRE WHILE BREAKING AMBUSH. THEY THEN CLEARED TO THE NORTH AND SPOTTED ARTY.

132202H MAY   27/134/58/80 GMGC WELLS, ABHC FAUGHT, PAT. OFF., UNITS PROCEEDING SOUTH ON THE VAM CO DONG RIVER RECEIVED ONE B-40 FROM EAST BANK VIC XS617720. UNITS RETURNED FIRE WHILE CLEARNING TO THE SOUTH. 81MM MORTAR PLACED IN THE AREA BY 2/50/25 ARVIN WHILE UNITS PROCEEDED SOUTH TO CHECK FOR POSSIBLE CROSSING. NEG. CROSSING.

140215H MAY   27/134   GMGC WELLS, PAT. OFF., UNITS IN WBA AT XS715625 OBSERED ONE VC WALKING ALONG BEACH ON EAST BANK. MAN PROCEEDED INTO WATER AND APPROACHED TO WITHIN 10 FEET OF BOATS AT WHICH TIME UNITS TOSSED TWO CONCUSSION GRENADES AND OPENED FIRE WITH M-16, KILLING HIM IMMEDIATELY. PATROL HELD FIRE UNTIL THEIR

DETECTION WAS IMMINENT BEFORE KILLING ENEMY AS HE APPEARED TO BE SCOUTING PRIOR TO A CROSSING ATTEMPT. ONE VC KIA(BC).

140830-140920H MAY   23/24 SM1 MANER, PAT. OFF., WHILE PATROLLING CLOSE TO THE WEST BANK AT XS715664 PATROL DETECTED THROUGH BREAKS IN THE FOLIAGE 10 PERSONS IN COLUMN FORMATION MOVING SOUTH. PERSONNEL EVADED INTO BUNKERS AND TALL GRASS WHEN THEY SPOTTED PBR'S. PATROL POSITIONED ITSELF ALONG BANK TO KEEP AREA UNDER SURVEILLANCE UNTIL CLEARANCE WAS GRANTED TO TAKE AREA UNDER FIRE. SEAWOLVES PUT A STRIKE IN THE AREA. UNK RESULTS.

141326H MAY   23/2 SM1 MANER, PAT. OFF., WHILE VISUALLY RECONNING AREA OF PREVIOUS CONTACT RECEIVED A/W FIRE FROM WEST BANK AT XS710665. PATROL --- NOT RETURN FIRE BECAUSE OF FRIENDLY TROOPS IN THE AREA. TROOPS WERE CONTACTED IN ORDER TO COORDINATE A SWEEP OF THE AREA BUT HAD TO LEAVE THE FIELD BEFORE SWEEP GOT TO THE ACTUAL AMBUSH SITE ON ORDERS FROM THEIR HIGHERS.

141550H MAY   23/24 SM1 MANER, PAT. OFF., IN SAME AREA WHERE PATROL HAD CONTACT EARLIER IN THE DAY, AT XS717662, THEY WERE TAKEN UNDER FIRE BY ONE B-40 AND A/W FIRE FROM WEST BANK. CLEARED THE AREA AND SPOTTED ARTY.

141634H MAY   25/153   BMC LEWIS, PAT. OFF., PATROL WHILE ESCORTING CRIPPLED T BOATS WERE TAKEN UNDER FIRE FROM BOTH BANKS AT XS584787 BY B-40 ROCKETS AND HEAVY A/W FIRE. ALL BOATS RETURNED FIRE AND CLEARED AREA. AIR OBSERVER WAS REQUESTED AND OVERHEAD WITHIN MINUTES TO SPOT ARTY.

142025H MAY   27/134   GMGC WELLS, PAT. OFF., UNITS IN WBA AT XS718645 DETECTED THROUGH NIPA PALM ABOUT 5 VC MOVING TOWARDS BOATS. ONE VC IN CLEAR WAS TAKEN UNDER FIRE BY CREWMEMBER WITH M-16 RIFLE WHILE TWO OTHER CREWMEMBERS TOSSED GRENADES ON ENEMY LOCATIONS. ONE GRENADE WAS THROWN IN RETURN BY VC BUT BLEW CLOSE ASTERN OF BOAT WITH NO DAMAGE DONE. ONE VC KIA (PROB).

151852H MAY   19/72 SMC BRYANT, PAT. OFF., ELEMENTS IN WBA AT XS677668 DETECTED TWO VC APPROACHING ON THE BANK. VC WERE TAKEN UNDER FIRE AND THE BANK RECONNED. PBR's CONTINUED AMBUSH IN SAME AREA IN HOPES OF CATCHING VC TRYING TO POLICE UP THE AREA. NEG RESULTS. TWO VC KIA (BC).

151907H MAY   27/134   GMGC WELLS, PAT., OFF., BOATS

PATROLLING SOUTH ON THE VAM CO DONG RIVER DETECTED AN EVADING SAMPAN AT XS707613. SAMPAN WAS MOVING FROM WEST BANK TOWARD EAST BANK AFTER AN UNKNOWN PATROL TRANSITING ON THE VAM CO DONG INTO VAM DO TAY PASSED. WHEN PATROL WAS SPOTTED THE SAMPAN IMMEDIATELY REVERSED COURSE AND BEACHED ON THE WEST BANK. OCCUPANTS SUCCESSFULLY EVADED INTO POPULATED AREA. ONE SAMPAN DESTROYED, MOTOR CAPTURED.

16130H MAY   27/134   GMGC WELLS, PAT. OFF., SIGHTED SAMPAN WITH TWO OCCUPANTS ENTERING SMALL CANAL FROM VAMCO DONG RIVER. FAC OVERHEAD REPORTED SIGHTING SAMPAN WITH OCCUPANTS AT APPROX SAME TIME. SAMPAN OVERTURNED AND OCCUPANTS EVADED INTO NEARBY BUNKER. FAC SPOTTED 40MM GRENADE FIRE PUT INTO AREA BY PATROL. ONE SAMPAN DESTROYED.

171939H MAY   23/24 SM1   MANER,   PAT.   OFF.,   WHILE PARTICIPATING IN OPERATION CAESAR II IN WBA AT XS591798 DETECTED MOVEMENT ON BEACH HEADING SOUTH TOWARDS USA POSITION 300 METERS AWAY. PATROL HELD FIRE DUE TO POSITION OF FRIENDLIES AND ATTEMPTED TO NOTIFY USA ELEMENTS BUT NOISE FROM RADIO FAN APPARENTLY ALERTED ENEMY TO BOATS' POSIT AND BOAT WAS TAKEN UNDER FIRE BY S/A AND GRENADES. PATROL RETURNED FIRE WITH S/A AND CLEARED THE AREA. ARMY ELEMENTS PROSECUTED CONTACT. RANBURGER, GMG3 WOUNDED. GMG3 SHOPE THREE GRENADE OVERBOARD.

181050-181250H MAY 58/80   ABHC FAUGHT, PAT., OFF. PATROL SPOTTED ONE VC CARRYING AK-47 EVADED INTO BUNKER AT XS575773, ARMY LHFT ARRIVED ON SCENE 1130H AND TOOK BUNKER UNDER FIRE. PBR'S EXTRACTED ONE SQUAD 1/4/12 FROM WEST BANK AND INSERTED THEM EAST BANK. SQUAD CHECKED BACK OF THE BUNKER CAVED IN AND SURMISED THAT VC HAD LEFT VAI BACK OF BUNKER.

181925H MAY   19/72 SMC BRYANT, PAT. OFF., IN WBA AT XS603772 HEARD MAN IN AREA MOVING TOWARDS PBR's. BECAUSE OF FRIENDLIES NEARBY, HE WAS CHALLENGED. AT THAT TIME MAN MADE A DASH TOWARDS BOAT. WE THREW GRENADES AT PERSON AND BROKE AMBUSH. ONE VC KIA (PROB).

182205H MAY   23/24 SM1 MANER, PAT. OFF., WHILE IN WBA AT XS589794 ON THE WEST BANK, PATROL DETECTED MOVEMENT TOWARD THEIR POSITION, UNITS THREW FRAG GRENADE AT VC KNEE DEEP IN WATER AND THEN TOOK HIM UNDER FIRE. OTHERS WERE HEARD RETREATING, BANK WAS NOT RECONNED BY FRIENDLY ELEMENTS OF OPERATION CAESAR II. PATROL BROKE AMBUSH, MOVED TO THE OPPOSITE BANK BELIEVING THE ENEMY

MIGHT TRY AGAIN. NEG RESULTS. ONE VC KIA(PROB).

191730-191800H MAY   58/80 ABHC FAUGHT, PAT. OFF. PATROL PARTICIPATING IN OPERATION CAESAR II, WHILE PROCEEDING SOUTH ON THE VAM CO DONG RIVER SIGHTED PERSONEL IN A FIELD VIC XS590773. BOATS NOSED INTO BANK, PERSONNEL DUCKED OUT OF SIGHT. AT 1800H WHILE OBSERVING THEM, UNITS SAW ONE MAN WEARING OLIVE DRAB SHIRT AND SHORTS AND CARRYING M-16. MAN SIGHTED UNITS AND BEGAN TO EVADE. WARNING SHOTS FIRED AND THEN MAN WAS TAKEN UNDER FIRE WITH M-16 AND 40MM. VNN MADE SEARCH OF THE AREA WITH NEG RESULTS.

192030H MAY   19/72 SMC   BRYANT,   PAT.   OFF.,   PATROL, PARTICIPATING IN OPERATION CAESAR II, IN WBA AT XS576777 OBSERVED 5VC APPROACHING THEIR POSITION, VC APPROACHED TO WITHIN 10 FEET OF BOATS AT WHICH TIME THEY WERE TAKEN UNDER FIRE WITH S/A. ONE BOAT BROKE AMBUSH AND RESET 100 MTRS NORTH. 3VC KIA (PROB).

202115-202300H MAY   23/24/25/153 BMC LEWIS, SM1 MANER, PAT. OFF., PATROLS, WHILE PARTICIPATING IN OPERATION CAESAR II, WITH SNIPER EMBARKED WERE IN WBA AT BANK, COVER BOAT HEARD PERSONNEL APPROACHING BOAT (MANER), WITH HAND COODINATION THROUGH LEAD BOAT, UPON SIGNAL, LEAD BOAT POPPED ILLUMINATION OVER MOVEMENT. WHEN ILLUM BROKE 14VC WERE CAUGHT IN THE OPEN MOVING TOWARD COVER BOAT. 2VC WERE CLOSE TO COVER BOAT, APPARENTLY WAKLING POINT FOR THE REST OF THE UNIT INLAND. THEY CAUGHT COMPLETELY BY SURPRISE, WERE TAKEN UNDER FIRE BY M-16 AND 40MM GRENADES BEFORE THEY COULD REACT AND 2VC NEAR COVER BOAT AND 3 OF THE ENEMY INLAND WERE SEEN TO FALL. ARTY, BLACK PONY AND FIREFLY STRIKES WERE PPUT INTO THE AREA.

210152-210630H MAY   23/24/25/153 BMC LEWIS, SM1 MANER, PAT. OFF., UNITS IN WBA, WHILE PARTICIPATING IN OPERATION CAESAR II, WERE REQUESTED BY USA TO CHECK THEIR AMBUSH POSITION   AT   XS595772   WITH   WHICH   THEY   HAD   NO COMMUNICATIONS.   AS   PATROL   WAS   INVESTIGATING, COMMUNICATIONS WERE ESTABLISHED IT WAS DETERMINED THAT ELEMENTS HAD BEEN OVERRUN AND EVERYONE KILLED OR WOUNDED. TWO PATROL PROVIDED A BLOCKING FORCE AND PUT IN AIR STRIKES AND TROOPS MADE A GROUND SWEEP, NEG RESULTS 5 USA KIA, 3 USA WIA.

212045H MAY   23/24 SM1 MANER, PAT. OFF., IN WBA DURING OPERATION CAESAR II WITH SNIPERS EMBARKED DETECTED MOVEMENT IN NIPA PALM ALONG THE BANK AT XS583770. WHEN PATROL THREW GRENADES ON MOVEMENT ONE VC WAS

OBSERVED RUNNING TO THE NORTH AND WAS TAKEN UNDER FIRE WITH 40M GRENADES.

212200H MAY   25/153   BMC LEWIS, PAT. OFF., PATROL IN WBA IN SUPPORT OF OPERATION CAESAR II WITH USA SNIPERS EMBARKED AT XS595767 RECEIVED A/W FIRE FROM SMALL GROUP ON VC MOVING TOWARD BANK. UNITS RETURNED FIRE AND RESET AMBUSH IN THE VICINITY BELIEVING THE VC WERE LOOKING FOR AN ESCAPE ROUTE THROUGH CORDON. RESULTS: 1 VC KIA (PROB).

212000H MAY   2-132-1   CDR SOTTAR, BMC COLLIER, PAT. OFF., RAS 13 UNITS IN SUPPORT OF OPERATION CAESAR II FIRING H&I WITH ZIPPO AND 105MM RECEIVED 4ORDS AK-47 FIRE FROM THE EAST BANK AT XS573770 WHILE PATROLLING NORTH. BOATS RETURNED FIRE AND CONTINUED PATROL. NEG FURTHER CONTACT.

221918H MAY   23/24/134   SM1 MANER, PAT. OFF., WHILE PREPARING TO SET UP IN WBA DURING OPERATION CAESAR II, PATROL WAS TAKEN UNDER FIRE BY 9 B-40 ROCKETS AND A/W FIRE FROM THE EAST BANK AT XS589785, ONE ROCKET HIT COVER BOAT (134). PATROL RETURNED FIRE AND CLEARED THE AREA. TWO MORE FIRING RUNS WERE MADE ON THE AMBUSH SITE. ARTY WAS REQUESTED BUT COULD NOT BE OBTAINED DUE TO FRIENDLY TROOPS IN THE AREA. GMG3 MENZIES WOUNDED ON LIP.

222015H MAY   58/80   ABHC FAUGHT, PAT. OFF., PATROL CONDUCTING A LAND/WATER COORDINATED AMBUSH WITH RECON PLT 5/60/9TH INF/. DIV., AT XS634703 MADE CONTACT WITH ABOUT 8 VC MOVING TOWARDS THE VAM CO DONG RIVER, RECON ELEMENT IN AMBUSH 100 METERS INLAND MADE INITIAL CONTACT WITH VC UNITS MOVING TOWARDS RIVER BANK AND TOOK THEM UNDER FIRE WITH A/W AS RECON ELEMENT MOVED BACK TO THE BOAT PBR PUT DOWN COVERING FIRE ON FLANKS. RECON ELEMENT WAS EXTRACTED AND REINSERTED 1 KILOMETER TO THE SOUTH. 2 VC KIA (BC).

232108H MAY   27/134   GMGC WELLS, PAT. OFF., IN WBA AT XS556816 DETECTED ABOUT 6 PERSONS APPROACHING BOATS AND ONE OTHER PERSON IN TREE NEAR BOATS. AT 2108 BOATS TOOK PERSONNEL UNDER FIRE AND CLEARED THE AREA. ONE FIRING RUN WAS MADE ON THE AREA. ARTY WAS REQUESTED BUT COULD NOT BE OBTAINED DUE TO FRIENDLIES IN THE AREA. 1 VC KIA (PROB).

240225H MAY   58/80   ABHC FAUGHT, PAT. OFF., IN LAND/WATER COORDINATED AMBUSH WITH RECON PLT FROM 5/60/9TH INF. DIV. AT XS627708 WHEN COVER BOAT WITH RECON

SQUAD IN CLOSE PERIMETER AROUND BOAT, HEARD 8-9 VC APPROACHING BOAT FROM INLAND. WHEN ENEMY WAS 15-20 METERS FROM PERIMETER, BOAT AND RECON ELEMENT TOOK ENEMY UNDER FIRE. FALSE EXTRACTION WAS MADE WITH NEW COMBINED AMBUSH SET 100 METERS SOUTH. NEG. FURTHER CONTACT. 1 VC KIA (BC), 2 VC KIA (PROB).

240828-241100H MAY   19/72 SMC BRYANT, PAT. OFF., INSERTED ONE PLATOON OF B/2/3/199TH LIB TO SWEEP AREA OF PREVIOUS CONTACT (SPOTREP#1746). ONE BOX OF CHICOM GRENADES WAS DISCOVERED.

241935H MAY   58/80 BMC COLLIER, PAT. OFF., IN LAND/WATER COORDINATED AMBUSH WITH RECON SQUAD 5/60/9TH INF. DIV. AT XS664675. UPON INSERTION TWO ENEMY WERE OBSERVED 20 METERS FROM THE RIVER BANK AND WERE TAKEN UNDER FIRE. HAVING DISCLOSED THEIR PRESENCE, RECON SQUAD WAS EXTRACTED AND AMBUSH WAS RESET.

242026-242116H MAY   27/134   GMGC WELLS, PAT, OFF., IN WBA AT XS575775 DETECTED AN ESTIMATED TWO SQUADS APPROACHING THEIR POSITIONS FROM TWO DIRECTIONS AN AIRBORNE PSYOPS SPEAKER MISSION WAS OBSERVED TAKING SOME FIRE FROM THE AREA. ARTY WAS REQUESTED FROM BEN LUC. UNITS BROKE AMBUSH WHILE RECONNING THE AREA AND THEN POSITIONED TO SPOT ARTY.

242110H MAY   27/134/SKIMMER LTJG SHANNON, GMGC WELLS, PAT. OFF., IN WBA AT XS596773 HEARD MOVEMENT BEHIND NIPA AT THEIR POSITION AND OBSERVED ONE MAN WALK TO A POINT OF LAND AT WE MOUTH OF A NEARBY STREAM AND THEN RETURN TO THE COVER OF THE NIPA. UNIT HEL FIRE BELIEVING THIS WAS A SECURITY GROUP FOR A SAMPAN CROSSING. NOISES CONTINUES AND AT 2150 ONE MAN AGAIN WALKED TO THE POINT OF LAND AND SPOTTED THE SKIMMER. UNIT TOOK HIM UNDER FIRE AT CLOSE RANGE AS HE RAN BACK INTO ME NIPA. TWO OMER ENEMY PERSONNEL WERE MEN TAKEN UNDER FIRE 10-15 METERS AWAY. AS UNIT CEASED FIRE .3-4 ROUNDS OF SMALL ARMS FIRE WERE RECEIVED FROM THE AREA AND AREA RECONNED BY SKIMMER AND TWO PBR'S. I VC KIA (BC)

242142H MAY   58/80 BMC COLLIER, PAT. OFF., IN LAND/WATER COORDINATED AMBUSH WITH RECON SQUAD FROM 5/60/9TH INF. DIV. AT XS634700 WHEN BOATS DETECTED, 4-6 ENEMY PERSONNEL. BOATS COORDINATED WITH GROUND UNITS, LOBBED GRENADES AT THE MOVEMENTS, BROKE AMBUSH AND RESET 100 METERS TO ME SOUTH.

242212H   25/153   BMC LEWIS, PAT. OFF., IN LAND/WATER COORDINATED AMBUSH WITH RECON SQUAD 5/60/9TH INF. DIV.

AT XS722651 DETECTED SAMPAN WITH THREE OCCUPANTS MOVING NORTH ALONG WEST BANK OF VAM CO DONG. WHEN SAMPAN WAS ALMOST AT PBR POSITION THEY TURNED AND STARTED TO CROSS TO THE EAST BANK. AT THIS TIME PATROL ILLUM. SAMPAN AND DROVE OCCUPANTS INTO WATER WITH SMALL ARMS FIRE. WITH RECON ELEMENT PROTECTING WEST BANK, PBR SUCCESSFULLY CAPTURED ALL 3 VC UNHARMED. 3 VC CIA, 2750 RDS 7.62 AK-47 AMMO, 50 B-40 BOOSTERS, 30 RDS 82MM MORTAR, 2 LBS DOS., AND 1 SAMPAN.

250015H MAY   58/80 BMC COLLIER, PAT. OFF., IN LAND/WATER COORDINATED AMBUSH WITH RECON SQUAD 5/60/9TH INF. DIV., AT XS633706. RECON ELEMENT DETECTED TWO VC ON BEACH BUT COULD NOT TAKE THEM UNDER FIRE DUE TO THEIR POSITION. BOATS TOOK THEM UNDER FIRE, AND GROUND UNIT THEN SWEPT THE AREA WITH NEG RESULTS.

252124-252330H MAY   58/80 BMC COLLIER., PAT. OFF. 9, IN LAND/WATER COORDINATED AMBUSH WITH ELEMNTS OF RECON SQUAD 5/60/9TH INF. DIV. AT XS650690 WHEN GROUND UNIT OBSERVED 4-6 VC MOVING TOWARDS THEIR POSITION. GROUND UNIT OPENED FIRE AT RANGE. OF 15 MTRS AND RECEIVED RETURN FIRE AT THE SAME TIME THE COVER BOAT RECEIVED A/W FIRE AND RECONNED WITH S/A TO GROUND UNITS FLANKS. ARTY WAS REQUESTED WHILE GROUND FORCE WAS EXTRACTED. PBR'S MADE TWO FIRING RUNS. ARTY THEN PUT IN. GROUND FORCE THEN REINSERTED TO MAKE SWEEP OF THE AREA. AT 2259H RECON UNIT CAME UNDER FIRE BY AN ESTIMATED 15 VC TO NORTH, EAST AND WEST OF THEIR POSIT. AND PBR'S DETECTED HEAVY MOVEMENT TO THE NORTH ALONG TREE LINES. PBR'S RECONNED TO NORTH AS RECON UNIT AGAIN WITHDREW TO THE BOATS AND WERE EXTRACTED PBR'S MADE FIRING RUNS, ARTY WAS CALLED IN AS WAS AN ARMY LEFT. 5 VC, KIA (BC) USA, I VC KIA (PROB) USN. TROOPS SWEEPING THE AREA THE NEXT DAY HAD I USA WIA BY BOOBY TRAP AND DESTROYED 10-12 BUNKERS.

262032H   27/134   GMGC WELLS, PAT. OFF., WHILE SETTING UP A LAND/WATER COORDINATED AMBUSH AT XS715635 WITH ELEMENTS OF THE 1ST PLT C/5/60/9TH INF. DIV. , A BOOBY TRAP NEAR THE BANK WAS TRIPPED BY THE GROUND ELEMENT AND I USA PERSONNEL SUFFERED SHRAPNEL WOUNDS TO LEFT LEG AND ANKLE. WIA DUSTED OFF.

270425H MAY   58/80 ABHC FAUGHT, PAT. OFF., IN A LAND/WATER COORDINATED AMBUSH WITH ELEMENTS OF C/5/60/9TH INF. DIV. AT XS667680 HEARD MOVEMENT AND SAW A LIGHT ON THE BEACH NEXT TO THE LEAD BOAT. BOAT, THREW TWO FRAG GRENADES AND 3 CONCUSSION GRENADES IN THE

DIRECTION OF THE MOVEMENT AND THEN PROCEEDED TO EXTRACT THE GROUND ELEMENT. NEG. RETURN FIRE RECEIVED.

281315-281800H MAY   23/24/19/72 SM1 MANER, PAT. OFF., SENT TO VIC XS600772 TO BLOCK AND . ASSIST 5/60/9TH INF. DIV. TROOPS IN HEAVY CONTACT. PATROL SET UP BLOCKING FORCE TO THE SOUTH OF CONTACT AREA AS FIXED WING, AND LHFT , AND ARTY STRIKES WERE PLACED IN THE AREA. CONTAC T CONTINUED: THROUGHOUT THE AFTERNOON AS PATROL HELPED EVACUATE WOUNDED CIVILIANS. PATROL PICKED UP TWO OLD WOMEN AND AN OLD MAN WHO GAVE AN INDICATION OF LOCATION OF VC/NVA. AS BOATS CLOSED BEACH TO INVESTIGATE THEY WERE TAKEN UNDER FIRE BY AK-47 FROM POSITIONS IN THE VILLAGE VIC XS601774. AFTER COORDINATION WITH USA, UNITS TOOK ONE HOOTCH UNDER FIRE WITH 40MM AND NO FURTHER FIRE WAS RECEIVED. AS GROUND CONTACT CONTINUED, BOATS EMBARKED I PLT FROM C/5/60/9TH AS A READY REACTION FORCE. GROUND FORCES RECEIVED NEG. FURTHER CONTACT THROUGHOUT NIGHT. 5 USA KIA, 3 USA WIA.

301100H MAY 23/24   SM1 MANER, PAT. OFF., ON ROUTINE PATROL DISCOVERED ONE DEAD VN MALE WITH BACK FLOATING IN THE VAM CO DONG VIC XS735635. PATROL STRIPPED MAN OF BACK AND CONTENTS OF POCKETS. DEATH DUE TO BULLET WOUND THROUGH THE LEFT TEMPLE. CONDITION OF THE BODY WAS GOOD. EVIDENTLY DEAD FOR LESS THAN 24 HRS. MAN WORE KHAKI SHIRT AND SHORTS.

311914H MAY 27/134/SKIMMER   LT. DECLERCQ, GMGC WELLS, PAT. OFF., WERE SENT TO VIC XS558828 TO ASSIST 2/3/199 LIB WHICH WAS RECEIVING INCOMING MORTAR. UNITS SPOTTED SAMPAN CROSSING RIVER EAST TO WEST AT XS563837 AND ADJUSTED ARTY INTO AREA SAMPAN EVADED TO.

312020H MAY   27/134   GMGC WELLS, PAT. OFF., IN WBA AT XS580795 DETECTED 6-8 PERSONNEL ON BANK IN THE WATER NEAR THEIR POSITION. TOOK AREA UNDER FIRE AND BROKE AMBUSH. 2 VC KIA (PROB).

The following roster and patrol report is based on reports submitted to the Commander River Division Five-Nine-One, during January – May, 1969.

1. PATROL OFFICERS

		Number of Patrols				
		01	02	03	04	05/69
LT	K. L. DECLERCQ	3	7	11	12	3
LT	T. P. FENNO		2	--	--	--
LT	B. L. McGHEE	3	--	--	--	--
LTJG	J. O. SHANNON	16	12	6	9	1
LTJG	A. C. BECK II	16	11	11	9	1
LTJR	J. D. BRAY	--	--	20	10	2
SMC	J. R. BRYANT	21	20	25	26	27
BMC	E. COLLIER	19	17	10	6	8
ABHC	R. C. FAUGHT	19	21	25	24	21
BMC	L. LEWIS	--	5	--	21	28
SM1	H. J. MANER	--	13	--	12	26
BM1	A. J. MEDLEY	18	18	13	--	--
BM1	J. H. PARRISH	--	--	--	10	3
QMC	H. A. STEPHAN	4	--	--	--	--
TM1	J. L. WARD	22	22	8	--	--
GMGC	L. NMN WELLS	--	17	--	25	24

2. BOAT CAPTAINS

		01	02	03	04	05/69
GMG2	R. CASTRO	--	5	24	9	--
SM1	R. C. DEDLEY	25	--	--	--	--
SM1	ENGLISH	14	--	--	--	--
EN2	D. C. HUTCHISON	--	9	--	--	--
EN2	R. C. KELLY	24	20	17	23	15
BM1	D. P. KUYKENDALL	--	15	25	27	29
EN1	J. R. LANE	4	9	24	28	23
SM1	H. J. MANER	--	22	--	--	
SM1	R. C. MEDLEY	25	9	25	--	
SM1	R. L. NEMMERS	7	--	--	--	
BM1	R. L. NUGENT	25	22	23	24	28
BM1	J. H. PARRISH	--	3	22	15	26
QM1	R. NMN RAMIREZ	5	23	24	25	29
BM3	K. E. REIMAN	19	2	7	11	8
BM1	A. L. RICHMOND	--	--	--	--	24

SM1 C. R. ROBERTS	7	20	16	9	17
BM1 W. NMN ROBINSON	--	--	--	25	25
QM1 D. E. ROTH	12	--	--	--	--
BM1 H. C. SALA	--	--	15	27	27
RD1 R. A. SEARS	--	--	--	27	25
EN1 R. P. STARK	24	22	14	1	--
GM2 W. D. WARNER	25	20	23	19	21
RD1 P. R. WILLIS	7	--	--	--	--

3. CREWMEN	01	02	03	04	05/69
ARMENDARIZ W. NMN	24	22	24	28	22
BLAKE, C. NMN	2	--	--	--	--
BUECHLER P. L., GMG3	26	20	20	23	25
CARTER R. L., SN	25	23	25	25	27
CHEW, W. A., BM3	--	--	24	23	26
DEAL, A. B., GMG2	24	22	16	5	20
EVANS, W. C.	13	--	--	--	--
FILSON, G. A., GMG3	--	--	--	--	14
FLOWERS, D. L.	21	--	--	--	--
GROSSE, D. A., EN2	--	--	--	17	29
HENSLEY, J. C., GMG2	25	22	22	25	19
HUTCHISON, D. C., EN2	10	--	--	8	11
KIMBLE, J. R., EN2	18	18	12	25	22
KOLENDA, R. L., SN	25	11	16	13	--
KRAMER, L. J., EN2	25	22	22	24	29
KUHN, D. R., PH3	24	21	4	2	2
KUSKMAN, L. A., EN2	26	22	24	26	29
LARSEN, L. E., EN2	24	22	22	26	18
LOGAN, B.	3	4	--	--	--
MARBUT, H. W., EN3	26	21	26	22	18
MARVIN, J. E., GMG3	27	20	26	21	1
MEADE, L. J., EN2	25	20	22	21	26
MENZIES, D. E., GMG3	25	20	2	2	25
MIGUES, H. J., EN2	25	22	15	--	8
NASH, J. B., SN	--	--	22	28	29
NELSON, S. A., GMG2	26	20	20	25	25
PARKS, G. L., GMGSN	--	17	27	28	30
PHILLIPS, C. R., ENFN	--	16	26	20	--
PITRE, D. NMN, GMG3	26	22	24	1	8
PRICE, P. W., EN2	25	21	21	28	29
RANBUGER, R. A.,GMG3	2_	21	27	26	16
ROSENBERG, K. L., GMGSN	--	--	--	25	--

SHOPE, P. H., GMG3	--	2	--	25	29
STANLEY, G. L., EN3	26	17	17	10	--
STEALER, J. L., GMG3	25	22	22	26	25
STOREY, J. E., GMG3	--	6	--	17	27
TERRY M. G., GMG2	25	22	11	4	21
THOMAS R. J., EN2	25	20	25	16	27
THOMPSON, B. C.	--	--	2	--	--
TREADWAY, T. NMN	--	19	22	--	--
VALENTINE, J. C., EN3	2	19	14	11	--
WESLEY, H. M., GMG3	--	--	16	26	27
WHITSEY, C. NMN, EN2	25	20	27	26	16
WILLIAMS, R. M., GMG3	25	20	24	15	--
WINCHELL, W. M.	25	18	--	--	--
WISER, T. L., GMG2	23	21	27	13	29
WOLF, C. B., GMG2	--	--	17	28	29
WORKMAN, D. L., SN	--	--	--	14	23
YANEZ, R. E., SN	--	--	--	15	29

BIBLIOGRAPHY

Anderson, Bern. *By Sea and by River. The Naval History of the Civil War*. New York: Da Capo, 1962.

"Boats of the Riverine Force."
http(=Internet)://www.cris.com/~sgt071/boats.htm

Croizat, Lt. Col. Victor, USMC (Ret.). *The Brown Water Navy. The River and Coastal War in Indo-China and Vietnam, 1948-1972*. Poole, Dorset: Blandford Press, 1984.

_____. *Vietnam River Warfare, 1945-1975*. London: Bradford Press, 1986.

Cutler, Thomas J., Lt. Cdr., USN. *Brown Water, Black Berets. Coastal and Riverine Warfare in Vietnam*. Annapolis: Naval Institute Press, 1988.

Dougan, Clark, Stephen Weiss, and the editors of Boston Publishing Company. *Nineteen Sixty-Eight. The Vietnam Experience*. Boston: Boston Publishing Company, 1983.

Frederickson, Gene W. and Brendan W. Tully. *River Patrol. The Game Wardens of Vietnam*. Narrated by Robert Stack. Color VHS Video. 1993.

Fulton, Maj. Gen. William B. *Riverine Operations, 1966-69*. Washington, DC: Department of the Army, 1973.

Hain, Tom. "The Mobile Riverine Force."
http(=Internet)://www.vietvet.org/hain.htm

Holley, Byron E., M.D. *Vietnam 1968-1969. A Battalion Surgeon's Journal*. New York: Ivy Books, 1993.

Kaiser, Charles. *1968 in America. Music, Politics, Chaos, Counterculture, and the Shaping of a Generation*. New York: Weidenfeld & Nicolson, 1988.

Ketwig, John. *....And a Hard Rain Fell. A GI's True Story of the War in Vietnam*. New York: Pocket Books, 1985.

Lowe, Alan L. "Buz." "The U.S. Navy patrol vessels of Task Forces 115, 116 and 117 played a key role in the war." *Vietnam* (Feb.,1996) : 12-57.

Marolda, Edward J. *By Sea, Air, and Land. An Illustrated History of the U.S. Navy and the War in Southeast Asia*. Washington, DC: Naval Historical Center, 1994.

Nelson, Capt. Carl A. USN (Ret.). "Controlling the Rung Sat Special Zone." *Vietnam* (Oct., 1996) :22-28.

Page, Dave. *Ships versus Shore. Civil War Engagements along Southern Shores and Rivers*. Nashville: Rutledge Press, 1994.

Rottman, Gordon L. *The Vietnam Brown Water Navy. Riverine and Coastal Warfare, 1965-69*. Hong Kong: Concord Publications, 1997.

Schreadley, Cdr. R.L., USN (Ret.). *From the Rivers to the Sea. The United States Navy in Vietnam*. Annapolis, Naval Institute Press, 1992.

_____. *The U.S. Navy in Vietnam*. Annapolis: United States Naval Institute, 1992.

Schwarztrauber, Comm. S.A., USN. "River Patrol Relearned." In: *Vietnam. The Naval Story*. Ed. Frank Uhlig, Jr. Annapolis: Naval Institute Press, 1986: 365-411.

Sheppard, Don. *Riverine. A Brown-Water Sailor in the Delta, 1967*. New York: Pocket Books, 1992.

Sweetman, Jack. *American Naval History: An Illustrated Chronology of the U.S. Navy and Marine Corps 1775-Present*. Annapolis, MD: Naval Institute Press, 1984.

"Vietnam Veterans' Home Page."
http(=Internet)://grunt.space.swri.edu/index.htm

Wintle, Justin. *Romancing Vietnam. Inside the Boat Country*. New York: Pantheon Books, 1991.

Witcover, Jules. *The Year the Dream Died. Revisiting 1968 in America*. New York: Warner Books, 1997.

Photo Album of
Darryl C. Hutchison, EN2, USN
a member of our boat crew

Command PBR and cover boat. Photo taken across the business end of our forward twin .50's.

A gathering of our crew around the chart, discussing a mission we had just been assigned.

Minesweeping boat [MSB] out of Nha Be on an early morning sweep of the Long Tao shipping channel, searching for mines that may have been set undetected the night before.

Something partially submerged floating on the Long Tao. A few select shots at it from a safe distance caused it to explode. The MSB boats had recently gone through on a mine sweep. Note the defoliated north bank near the river.

A view from the river of the south side of Nha Be village near the base compound.

A small village on the Long Tao in the Rung Sat. Our patrol picked up a South Vietnamese soldier and his pregnant wife here and delivered them to Nha Be just in time.

Cover boat alongside for a conference.

Sunset on the Long Tao River in the Forest of Assassins. What awaits us tonight?

Sampan traffic was busiest early in the morning and late in the evening.

Often we were observed. Was it Charlie without his weapons, looking for a weakness?

PCF on the Long Tao, We called him "Perky Bear Foxtrot."

Nha Be pier, PCF taken out of the water for repairs.

Our reception party at Can Gio when we delivered several South Vietnamese soldiers there. They left a surprise for us in our boat's grenade locker.

A forward air controller aircraft flying low and close to us over the southern part of the Long Tao River. These were often hit by small arms ground fire.

The radio antennas had to be lowered to let the seawolves make a helicopter-to-boat transfer of one man to PBR 72.

Tango boats and Monitors on one of the streams we patrolled in the Rung Sat.

A few shots put into the stream that was called "The Hanging Tree" on the Long Tao. Most trees and foliage had been blown away with artillery and rocket strikes.

PBR #72 at full speed, our cover boat on our starboard quarter.

A baby crocodile one of the guys came up with. We kept him a couple days, but he would not eat our c-rations so we had to let him go.

Nha Be Base compound

Local homes on the south side of the river below Nha Be.

Water Buffalo often seen near the narrow short cut canal south of Nha Be. The canal was used only during daylight hours for safety reasons.

A water taxi on the Long Tao slowing for us to come alongside, board it and check out it's passengers and cargo.

Smiles came easy for many of the children.

We were a source of amusement for some.

And fear for others.

The PBR on which Sampan Smith [Theodore Smith, QMC, USN], and several of his men were killed. Note the extensive rocket and bullet damage in these photos.

Our PBR that was hit at the Hanging Tree firefight out of the water for repairs.

Sometimes a PBR was sunk and had to be fished out.

Activity around the Ben Luc bridge. A view from the bridge of
the *USS Harnett County*.

190

Rag boats [River Assault Group] coming down the Vamco Dong from the direction of Tra Cu, another Charlie hot spot just right out of Cambodia.

One of our new homes on the sand-filled swamp at Ben Luc.

It's good to be back "home" after a long hard day on the river.

The monsoon rains forced us to cover our weapons if we did not feel threatened.

A small village alongside one of the small streams we patrolled.

The search for contraband and suspected VC continues daily.
Sometimes it resulted in detaining some and delivering them
to the South Vietnamese compound for interrogation.

A typical sampan search.

Into the night we go, not knowing what it holds for us.

SMC Jimmy R. Bryant, USN